EFFECTIVE SHORT-TERM COUNSELLING WITHIN THE PRIMARY CARE SETTING

EFFECTIVE SHORT-TERM COUNSELLING WITHIN THE PRIMARY CARE SETTING

Psychodynamic and Cognitive–Behavioural Therapy Approaches

Valerie Garrett

KARNAC

First published in 2010 by
Karnac Books Ltd
118 Finchley Road, London NW3 5HT

British Library Cataloguing in Publication Data

A C.I.P. for this book is available from the British Library

ISBN: 978 1 85575 751 6

Edited, designed and produced by The Studio Publishing Services Ltd
www.publishingservicesuk.co.uk
e-mail: studio@publishingservicesuk.co.uk

www.karnacbooks.com

CONTENTS

To my husband Peter, my daughters Jackie, Maria, and Kirstie,
and my grandchildren Vicky, Camilla, Jack, and Abby
for their love, support, and encouragement.

ACKNOWLEDGEMENTS

I wish to thank Anne Waldock and Patrick Baker for patiently proof-reading my manuscript, Trevor Waldock for advice on getting published, and Jonathan Waldock for technical support. Thank you to Anne Wedd for valuable CBT and IT support and advice. To Val Potter and Pat Seber for reading my final manuscript and for their helpful comments. Thank you Susan Baker and John Bridge for essential practical help. To all my colleagues for giving me the privilege and satisfaction of supervising their primary care case work.

ABOUT THE AUTHOR

Valerie Garrett has been a psychodynamic counsellor for over twenty-five years. She holds an MA in supervision of counselling and psychotherapy. Valerie worked as a primary care counsellor for five years in a GP practice from 1989–1994. Since 1994 to the present, she has supervised the casework of counsellors and trainees on placement in GP practices and clinics.

HOW TO USE THIS BOOK

The reader can dip into or read this book straight through as appropriate to their need.

At the end of each chapter is a summary of key issues that are essential to good practice within the primary care setting.

The book is in two parts, the first part appertaining to the understanding of the intrapersonal and interpersonal dynamics of the primary care personnel and the impact of the setting on the counsellor and his/her work. It looks at the patient's relationship with the holding and containing elements of the whole primary care environment.

Part II looks at assessment for both psychodynamic and CBT short-term counselling. It then moves on to the "how" of the counselling, using these two approaches or an integration of both. It looks at the "how" in relation to different types of patient and presenting problems, for example, very young, elderly, bereaved, etc. For instance, one would not use a short-term psychodynamic approach with someone who is recently bereaved or a purely CBT approach with someone in crisis. Part II also looks at the different ways in which distress and pathology manifest themselves. In the primary care setting, because of the broad intellectual, socio-economic, developmental, and personality spectrum of the patient population, it is often necessary to tailor-make a six-week contract using an integrative approach.

Why and for whom this book was written

In 1989, after training as a psychodynamic counsellor and supervisor, I was given the opportunity to become employed as a counsellor in a GP surgery. I soon realized that, for the short-term model of counselling that was the norm in primary care, I would need to develop a far more eclectic approach.

The nature of counselling in primary care is different from any other setting. The distress and problems that the patients present are varied and often complex, but the amount of counselling time that each patient may receive is limited. The provision of short-term counselling in this setting calls upon the counsellor to utilize all the models, methods, and techniques at their disposal.

GPs value the counsellors in their employ, and many more are now needed to satisfy the growing demand. This book is written for the counsellor who is seeking to work in primary care and the trainee on, or intending to secure, their clinical placements in that setting. It aims to bridge the gap between all that they know already and what will be expected of them in this challenging setting.

When I handed over to a colleague the teaching of trainee psychodynamic counsellors working towards their diplomas, I felt I still had a lot to offer. I have written this book to offer the reader access to my own experiences of counselling primary care patients, and supervising surgery counsellors and trainee counsellors in their clinical placements.

The book will appeal to both trained and trainee psychodynamic, cognitive–behavioural (CBT), and integrative counsellors who wish to use their skills effectively and gain knowledge and understanding of the unique properties and variables of the primary care setting.

It is written in an easy to read style and format that may enable GPs and other primary care staff to gain insights into their unique environment and to obtain a better understanding of the counsellor's role and skills.

Why now?

Improving Access to Psychological Therapies (IAPT)

Under new government guidelines, many more counsellors and psychological therapists will be needed. Speaking at the Psychological Therapies in the NHS Conference, Health Secretary Andy Burnham renewed the government's commitment to completing the roll-out of IAPT. The progress across the country has been encouraging. The British government is committed to increasing access to talking therapies and has requested that the NHS commission 3600 newly trained therapists. CBT therapists will form a major part of that commissioning, as CBT has shown practice-based evidence that it can be successful. Initially, two IAPT initiative pilot programmes were run in Newham and Doncaster. Following their success, a further fifty-two new IAPT sites were launched before March 2010, bringing the total number of IAPT sites to 115 (www.iapt.uk 30/11/09 www.bps.org.uk 2/11/09). Andy Burnham stressed the increasing number of job opportunities that will be created and funding released for new talking-therapy "Pathfinder" projects to allow people with anxiety and depression better access to psychological therapies (www.guardian.co.uk/society/joepublic/2009/dec/09/mental-health-services-policy). These "Pathfinders" point the way to a radical overhaul of mental health services with a much greater focus on creating access to talking therapies that ensure people are supported to make a rapid and sustainable recovery (*Healthcare Counselling and Psychotherapy Journal*, 2007, p. 2).

A positive practice guide to increasing access to psychological therapies has also been launched. *Commissioning a Brighter Future: Improving Access to Psychological Therapies—Positive Practice Guide* (Department of Health, 2007) explains why the British government is committed to talking therapies, and highlights examples of best practice from across England.

The New Savoy Declaration

In December 2007, the leaders of twenty health organizations united to declare their support for the government's efforts to offer timely access to psychological therapies on the NHS for all who need them. Joining together for the first national Psychological Therapies in the NHS Conference at Savoy Place, London, the twenty groups agreed the New Savoy Declaration, which states:

> Depression and anxiety affect millions of people in the UK, yet few receive the psychological therapies that could help with recovery. Many with the courage to seek help have to wait for many months for treatment or have to pay for it privately.
>
> The Government has committed itself to turning this around and to implementing NICE Guidelines for depression and anxiety so that everyone can have timely access to state-of-the-art evidence-based therapies. [Savoy Declaration, 2007, p. 9]

The Department of Health has pledged increased funding for its Improving Access to Psychological Therapies programme, rising from £30 million in 2008–2009 to £102 million in 2009–2010 and £170 million in 2010–2011 (Savoy Declaration, 2007).

Staff at the British Association for Counselling and Psychotherapy (BACP), which is recognised by legislators, national and international organizations, and the public as the leading professional body and the voice of counselling and psychotherapy in the UK, recently made a submission to a House of Commons Select Committee inquiry for the National Institute for Health and Clinical Excellence (NICE). Nancy Rowland, BACP's Head of Research, in collaboration with colleagues, produced the submission that relates to psychological therapies as delivered in the NHS, and focuses on the NICE evaluation process and whether any particular groups are disadvantaged by the process, the implementation of NICE guidance (which guidance is acted on, which is not, and the reasons for this), and why NICE's decisions are increasingly being challenged (Rowland, 2007).

I include a selection of findings from the executive summary of the submission that are relevant to the remit of this book. The selection, I believe, highlights the need for counselling from more than one theoretical model to take place in primary care, hence my majoring upon psychodynamic and CBT approaches.

The summary submits that psychological therapies are an important part of the delivery of health care within the NHS, and that they are highly valued by patients who increasingly choose counselling and psychotherapy in preference to medication. I back this with my own experience, both as a counsellor in a GP surgery and as supervisor for counsellors in that setting. I have found that it is often younger patients (aged forty-five and under) who want to try counselling without medication as a first choice.

The submission found that as mental health research is seriously under-funded, there has been limited systematic review and randomized controlled trial (RCT) evidence for the efficacy of psychological therapies for a range of conditions, with the exception of CBT. Therefore, many psychological therapies are left unevaluated by RCT. For this reason it has been argued that it is more appropriate for counselling and psychotherapy research to be based on the accumulation and analysis of practitioner-generated case studies, and, to this end, new approaches to case study research have been developed by Elliot (2002) and Stiles (2003). What is lagging behind is a way of researching evidence of the outcomes of other therapies, including the psychodynamic approach and the humanistic approaches such as person-centred counselling.

The UKCP Research Committee sees the importance for increased collaboration between researchers and practitioners, and has started a process of developing proposals for new forms of research programmes that involve practitioners directly with researchers in teams or networks. These are called Practitioner Research Networks. Sheila Butler, in the UKCP's journal *Psychotherapist*, sees this move as a particularly timely focus given the likelihood of statutory regulation (Butler, 2007). Research methods and approaches are still limited when evidence of therapeutic effectiveness is only collected using standard symptom-orientated measures, such as CORE, rather than complementing these with methods more concerned with changes in meaning, such as qualitative approaches or repertory grid techniques (Winter, 2003). Liddle and Frank (2006) think that clinical research activity in the field is more clinically and policy relevant than ever before, and that research-based therapies seem here to stay.

NICE guidelines exist to support delivery of psychological therapies across a range of mental health conditions, including depression and anxiety. My colleague and I, when conducting our own in-house research in the GP surgery, found that approximately 30% of referrals from GPs were for depression and/or anxiety.

It has been my experience that counsellors working in primary care are working at "the coalface", being referred patients with a range of mental health issues, including psychosis, as well as bereavement issues, relationship problems, social problems, and personality disorders. To merely rely upon evidence-based models of therapy may disadvantage the patient who needs a different approach, and does not fit neatly into a diagnostic category. I deal with this more fully in later chapters of the book.

BACP recommends that NICE review its evidence evaluation process to include quantitative and qualitative evidence when evaluating psychological therapies, including highly controlled studies, case studies, and effectiveness studies.

There is evidence that the quality of the therapist–patient relationship is relevant to the efficacy of treatment. Roth and Fonagy (1996) put forward that RCT evidence tends to focus on the type of treatment rather than the person giving it.

Why short-term counselling?

The optimal length of treatment has been a contentious issue since the time of Freud, and the debate continues to this day. I will not be entering into this debate in the text, since I am concerned more with what is than what might be. Counselling in NHS primary care will always have monetary constraints placed upon it, so we must make a "good enough" job with the skills and tools that we have. Long-term therapy or counselling is not widely available to most people because it is expensive and, therefore, for some, totally inaccessible.

Dryden and Feltham (1992) suggest that there is some evidence that brief therapy is as effective as long-term therapy and the reality is that therapy is invariably brief because that is what people want or can tolerate.

One model does not fit all

My experience of primary care counselling has taught me that one model does not fit all patients, and it would seem that we must sometimes decide between short-term and long-term gain when considering effectiveness of therapy in primary care.

The primary care setting is a fertile ground for investigating longer-term outcomes, as its patients are, in the main, a captive group. Patients have the opportunity to return more often for subsequent short-term contracts when new problems arise in their lives. In my experience, there is more likely to be long-term gain from short-term counselling when the patient is assessed as ready and able to benefit from short-term CBT or brief psychodynamic counselling. These patients are able, with help, to find a focus or goal for the counselling and are motivated to change. However, I have found that many patients would be assessed as not ready or able to make use of these methods, in their purer form, as they are more in need of supportive empowerment. This is expanded upon later in the book.

Often, GPs are not trained to assess a person's readiness for counselling or which type of counselling intervention would be most beneficial to them. A referral to the surgery counsellor for assessment can thus facilitate the most suitable referral. As the counselling system stands at present in the UK, this referral could be for counselling within the surgery for short-term intervention (for example, brief CBT, brief psychodynamic based or supportive counselling), back to the GP for a referral to the Community Mental Health Team or psychiatrist, or to the private sector.

There are private and charitable counselling agencies who offer sliding fee scales and private counsellors and psychotherapists who can be accessed through the BACP office or website. However, most counsellors and psychotherapists in primary care would hold information on what is available and affordable in their local area.

It is important that we, as primary care counsellors, do not lead patients or doctors into thinking that what we offer can help when we know it cannot. We are in post to offer care and protection within the remit of our work, and one of the most harmful ways in which we can serve patients is to fail to render needed therapy or to mislead about efficacy. Other types of injuries, as seen by Gray (2007c), are failure to refer a client to another service they may need; the creation of an unhealthy dependency that is difficult to resolve; confusing the client about the distinction between therapy and personal issues; and, in some cases, interference in family relationships and friendships so that the client becomes isolated. The above breaches of trust can provoke anger, loss of self-esteem, and self-confidence or depression.

Why psychodynamic and CBT models?

Face-to-face counselling in any counselling setting involves a relationship between a counsellor and a client. Relationship is a powerful tool no matter what theoretical model is practised. Psychodynamic and CBT both involve a relationship between counsellor and patient. Both models are carried out within the agreed time and place boundaries that are available within primary care. Short-term counselling, using either model, generally requires the counsellor to be more active, directive, and therapeutically challenging than when practising long-term counselling. The two models differ in the manner in which they are actively carried out. Within the broad patient base of primary care, some patients respond better to one approach and some to another.

At present, there is a move towards CBT counselling being the favoured model in primary care. However, there are many psychodynamic, integrative, and person-centred counsellors already employed within this setting all over the UK. As mentioned earlier, my main theoretical model is psychodynamic, but, over the years, I have integrated elements of the CBT approach into my counselling style when it has seemed helpful. However, it has also been appropriate to practise brief psychodynamic counselling with many patients. Some people seem "ripe" for this kind of work and are often self-aware and have insight into their personal problems, but may be temporarily fragile due to their present circumstances, be they relational or due to other factors out of their control, such as redundancy, ill health, death of a loved one, etc. With other patients, who are less self-aware, have less insight into their problems, and are emotionally more fragile, I have found it appropriate to use my psychodynamic thinking to understand their relational dynamics, but use the more structured approach of CBT, with its use of "homework" or trying out different thoughts and behaviours between sessions. The person may then achieve a greater sense of mastery and control as they experience "doing" something to help their problem in a concrete way.

Central to CBT is a focused effort to look at and change ways of thinking and behaving that have not satisfactorily worked to the patient's advantage. An attempt is made to enhance the patient's autonomy of thought and action, and therapists work with patients to free rigid thinking. A patient's self-belief systems and thoughts are investigated to facilitate them going forward with confidence rather than with a defeatist attitude. Some patients like the idea of planned step-by-step goals and achievements. Having understood how he/she thinks and behaves through a short-term CBT contract in a GP surgery, the patient may then move on from primary care into longer, deeper counselling elsewhere (depending upon what is available) where they may look at their underlying beliefs and modify them through long-term CBT counselling.

CBT is an active problem-solving approach that helps the patient to develop skills and enables them ultimately to become their own therapist. It focuses on the present and current problems and ways in which the patient's thinking and acting perpetuate the problems. Errors in thinking distort the facts, and CBT can help a patient step back and take another look at what they are thinking and attempt to make suitable corrections.

Loss, abuse, and neglect in childhood involve relationships, and beliefs about self and others laid down at this time are often negative and destructive. This can lead to mistrust or avoidance in relationships later in life.

These two models and their possible integration have been chosen because the patient base of the primary care setting is both broad and immediate. This breadth of patient base stems from the fact that most people in this country, at some time in their lives, attend and seek help from a GP surgery. Immediacy stems from the close physical proximity of the referrer, GP, nurse, etc., and the surgery counsellor. In some instances, the patient may simply walk from one end of the corridor to the other if a GP deems the situation to be urgent and the counsellor is available. In this instance, the person's problem is undoubtedly immediate and a counsellor is unlikely to turn anyone away once a referral has been made.

I consider a short-term counselling style that uses both psychodynamic thinking alongside CBT structure, with its emphasis on cognitions as well as feelings, brings both breadth and immediacy into creative and useful juxtaposition.

Key issue

Whatever the model or approach, it is often the counsellor's trust in the power of relationship and their own relevant intuitions that can be, for some people receiving counselling, the only way to hold on to hope

"When a doctor tells me that he adheres strictly to this or that method, I have my doubts about his therapeutic effect ... I treat every patient as individually as possible, because the solution of the problem is always an individual one ... A solution which would be out of the question for me may be just the right one for someone else"

(C. G. Jung, 1982, pp. 152–153)

PART I

THE PRIMARY CARE SETTING: FINDING YOUR FEET AT THE "COALFACE"

"There can be few other sectors of counselling provision that have experienced so much change and turbulence in such a short time"

(Mellor-Clark, 2000, p. 158)

1

Introduction to Part I

"Do we believe that a frightened, confused or overwhelmed person is 'ill' and requires medical treatment? . . . Distress is not an illness. To insist that distressed people are ill adds insult to injury, and diverts attention from the real causes of distress"

(Sanders, 2007, pp. 8–10)

Within this text, the terms "primary care setting" and "GP surgery" are used synonymously, as it is in these settings that that primary care counselling normally takes place. I use the terms "client" and "patient" interchangeably, and "therapist" and "counsellor" also. I explain any technical terms where necessary. All case studies and scenarios are disguised to protect the confidentiality and privacy of patients.

People and relationships

This book is about people and relationships. Human relationship forms the crucible in which emotional and developmental change

3

can happen; words are often the therapeutic medium of the work. We each have to hold our own state of equilibrium, and sometimes that equilibrium becomes shaken and fragile. For some, their equilibrium is always fragile and in permanent need of support of one kind or another. When we sit in front of our patient in the primary care setting, we do well to remind ourselves that "there, but for the grace of God, go I". We may be able to acknowledge to ourselves that we have indeed been on a similar journey to that of the patient and not merely survived it, but emerged a more whole person. We are still journeying.

Armstrong, in her book *The Bible, The Biography*, reminds us,

> Human beings are meaning-seeking creatures. Unless we find some pattern or significance in our lives, we fall very easily into despair. Language plays an important part in our quest. It is not only a vital means of communication, but it helps us to articulate and clarify the incoherent turbulence of our inner world. [Armstrong, 2007, p. 1]

The broad nature of the contents of this book reflects the broad spectrum of human distress and conflict that the reader will encounter when counselling in the primary care setting. The counselling work in this setting is carried out under the conditions of immediacy and short-term contracts, where beginnings and endings dominate the process.

Finding a secure launch pad for this book

While writing the first draft of this book, I must have been unconsciously looking for a secure launch pad from which to propel it upon its journey, and, by the end of that draft, I had found it. At least, I had found several sound components from which to construct that launch pad.

The relative stability and security of the primary care setting

An important component is the relative stability and security that people find in the National Health Service (NHS) primary care setting of this country. So much so, that the only ending with that environment that the patient is compelled to undergo is at the point of death. The patient's relationship with the NHS is "from the cradle to the grave". It is because of this long-term relationship of the patient with the primary care environment that the counsellor has a unique insight at the time of assessment into the attachment style of the patient: secure or insecure (avoidant, ambivalent, etc.). Adult attachment style is related to interpersonal behaviour and is predictive of ability to function both within intimate relationships and within work (Hazan & Shaver, 1990). A person's ability to trust both doctor and counsellor will depend upon their attachment style, and this, in turn, may have an impact upon how much use they are able to make of short-term counselling. If they were able to make secure attachments with their care-givers in childhood, their ability to withstand the vicissitudes of life and relationships will have sure foundations.

The creation of another important component or basis for exploration was sparked by four questions posed by Freeth (2007):

- Can those who see their practice as primarily relational, work within therapy settings built on the medical model?

- Are there ways of working alongside the medical model without compromising one's own values, or are the potential conflicts and contradictions too great to overcome?

- Can we uphold a view that therapy is an art while its practice along scientific principles is so dominant?

- Can non-medical model therapies survive within healthcare settings, and if so, can they put the heart back into health care? (Freeth, 2007, p. 7)

The medical model represents a particular way of explaining problems or pathology and Freeth (*ibid.*) sees this explaining disturbance in terms of a biological (disease) process in which there is a breakdown of the normal biological mechanism. It usually relies upon a set formula, assessment, diagnosis, and treatment. In mental health terms, she suggests this translates as a faulty mental mechanism, for example, depressed mood being the result of a biochemical imbalance. She believes that reliance upon biochemical explanations is the dominant paradigm within NHS primary care and mental health services, partly explaining the heavy use of psycho-tropic drugs for mental disorders.

When counselling in a primary care setting, whether the coun-sellor's approach is cognitive–behaviour therapy (CBT) or psycho-dynamic therapy, they are working in a setting where a path needs to be steered between the medical model and the talking therapy model. This ability to steer a path cannot be taught, but comes with experience. The counsellor will be at the helm of a well-made vessel, but will be sailing in a stormy sea and must keep their eye on their relational compass, the vessel being the counsellor's theo-retical model and clinical experience and the stormy sea being the unique variables of the different boundaries of the setting and the interpersonal relationships within the primary care team.

Bower (2007) puts forward that, "There is no real reason why psychotherapy should have anything to fear from the medical model. There are many systematic reviews and trials that show that psychotherapy is effective" (p. 19).

Often, it is the patient that brings a medical-model view of them-selves into the counselling room, especially if they have had no experience of counselling in the past. Therefore, it is important that we "embrace what is there" (Soth, 2007, p. 20) and work with it, rather than set ourselves in opposition to the medical-model way of operating. In this way, we do not deprive other helping and medical professionals of our psychological and relational awareness.

With the processes of assessment, diagnosis, and treatment being at the heart of the medical model and CBT, which can make it a mismatch with relationship-centred psychological therapies, the psychodynamic counsellor will need to decide whether they can, or want to, work within an organization that is dominated or signifi-cantly influenced by it.

The chosen models: CBT and psychodynamic approaches

Where a primary care setting has counselling as one of its services to the patient, it is often carried out using a short-term contract. A common model is assessment plus six ongoing fifty-minute sessions. This arrangement may vary between Primary Care Trusts (PCTs) throughout the country.

Short-term CBT therapy

The notion of "treatment" sits well within the medical model, with its measurable outcomes over the short term. Because CBT is an evidence-based therapy, it is highly favoured in our political climate. However, measures of longer-term outcomes do not put CBT ahead of other talking therapies.

Aaron Beck, founder of cognitive therapy, encourages a therapeutic perspective, where patient and counsellor work on "being scientific together" (in partnership) when approaching thought, feeling, and behavioural patterns (Willson & Branch, 2006).

Behavioural therapies are based upon learning theory that starts from the premise that there are many ways that learning can take place. Changing behaviour can lead to changes in thoughts, feelings, sensations, and the dynamics of relationships. We each have unique thought patterns and belief systems, which, when modified or changed, can affect our feelings and behaviour. An important concept for anyone to take on board is that hard as it is for us to change ourselves, it is easier than trying to change someone else!

By discovering what a person's goals and beliefs are in life, a counsellor can help them to feel more in control of their life as they begin to see that they have choices.

Short-term CBT aims to help people change patterns of thinking or behaviour that are causing problems to themselves or to other people in their lives. Changing how a person thinks and behaves can also change how a person feels. CBT is a structured approach, where goals are agreed between therapist and patient. Different behaviours and ways of thinking are tried out and practised during and between sessions. Any strong emotions experienced can be contained within the counselling relationship in the sessions, which can, in turn, help the person contain emotions between sessions.

Relationship is key to change. Both short-term CBT and psychodynamic counselling occur in a relationship between two people, in a collaborative partnership. Similar to psychodynamic assessment, the CBT counsellor makes a developmental formulation, which is shared with the patient. This may enable the patient to see how their past has coloured their present thinking, behaving, and feelings in their relationships, including that with the counsellor.

CBT can be seen as the "outside-in" approach to therapy. With CBT, we begin with the patient's life problems in the present. It is by facilitating a change in a person's present negative thoughts, feelings, and behaviours that can affect change in a person's life. It is recognized that these have been laid down in childhood and are controlled by unconscious beliefs. These unconscious beliefs influence a person's thoughts, causing them to have negative automatic thoughts (NATs). One aim of the counselling is to identify the person's unique set of negative automatic thoughts (and the resulting feelings and behaviours) and to challenge these habitual thought and behaviour patterns, using Socratic questioning, in order to facilitate a change. Socratic questioning is a gentle, yet persistent, enquiry with the patient in order to reach a real understanding of what it is like to live their life and what gives it meaning.

This way of working requires motivation on the part of the patient. If the patient is not sufficiently motivated, for whatever reason, the therapy will be less successful.

The NHS has a preference for CBT, which has the National Institute of Clinical Excellence (NICE) seal of approval because it can show evidence-based practice and, therefore, fits more happily within the medical model. I, too, have come to recognize that CBT, practised with carefully selected patients, can sit well within the remit of talking/psychological therapies. Some primary care practices have installed CBT programmes to be used on a computer without the presence of a therapist. These are normally used over a set number of sessions, usually at weekly intervals. This face-to-screen, rather than face-to-face, CBT counselling approach suits some patients and can work effectively with people who are strongly motivated to change and can use the time between sessions constructively to try out new ways of thinking and evaluate them in the light of their lives and relationships.

The way in which CBT is practised continues to change in the light of new research and, as there is a shortage of CBT counsellors, the government is promoting an extensive training initiative in the context of the "Increasing Access to Psychological Therapies" programme (IAPT). Many centres for counsellor training are offering CBT courses as an add-on to the counsellor or clinical psychologist's main training and theoretical base. This will give primary care counsellors an extra dimension when offering a counselling contract to meet the individual needs of the patient.

Short-term psychodynamic counselling

Short-term psychodynamic counselling can be seen as an "inside-out" approach to therapy. A thorough assessment looks at the patient's story, observing and considering both the patient's past and their present relational situation. From this information, a formulation is made based upon a hypothesis of the person's intrapsychic dynamics (internal world) and their links with past and present relationships. Through this process of psychodynamic formulation, a focus may be found for the short-term counselling contract.

The counsellor will be looking for a person's internal conflicts laid down in their psyche and personality during their formative years in their family of origin. This "family" may not be of a conventional nature (e.g. father, mother, and children), but will be those people with whom the person was raised through infancy and childhood.

The mode of expression of the basic internal conflicts may vary according to the social, economic, and cultural background of the patient, but the conflicts remain the same for any and all patients (Mann, 1973). These "core conflicts", as Mann refers to them, for example, independence *vs.* dependence or activity *vs.* passivity, which are dominating the person's life and causing distress, often become the focal point of the counselling.

It may be observed during the assessment how the person projects his/her inner world dynamics on to their present outside world and relationships. However, this may not become apparent during the assessment, but may manifest in subsequent sessions.

Similarly to short-term CBT, psychodynamic counselling is often about the counsellor using the tool of gentle challenge. It is the person's reaction or response to this in the session that is the material to be worked with. This material will contain important elements of the person's past ways of dealing with their life and relationships. In this way, the person's past experience of relationships that is transferred to the present relationship within the counselling room becomes another working tool for the counsellor.

CBT and psychodynamic counselling can empower a person in ways that may not have occurred before in their life. Provision of this nurturing setting, whichever approach is adopted, can provide fertile ground for the patient in which personal growth and understanding may be facilitated.

Not all patients are neatly served by one of the above approaches on its own, but this book looks at many scenarios that can be thought about and accommodated within a psychodynamic and/or CBT approach.

Always remember that the patient holds the key to a helpful outcome, and it is often the relationship between counsellor and patient that, as much as anything else, determines how far along their journey to experiencing less distress they may manage to achieve.

In short-term counselling, the counsellor's task may merely be to facilitate the person towards beginning their counselling journey, but it is often their experience of this first step which determines whether they go on to seek appropriate help in the community.

If you feel that in any given situation you have got about as much to offer as a sow's ear, just wait to see the silk purse that the patient can make of you!

The importance of a person's willingness to change

For short-term psychodynamic and CBT to be effective, the patient must be able to show a willingness to change. It is useful, therefore, to spend some time with the patient identifying the secondary gain or pay-off that they derive from their problems or symptoms. The person often needs help to see that perhaps some underlying basic need may be being met, albeit in a way that can make relationships difficult. For example, a person may become very angry and resentful within relationships where they feel controlled, belittled, or not considered in decision making. However, the basic need that is being met to some extent in those situations is that they never have to take action or responsibility for themselves; that is, their unmet dependency needs interfere with normal adult functioning.

We must remember that in this setting we are looking out for, and must listen to, what is true and meaningful for the patient before us. Without this humane approach, we are in danger of reducing what we do to mere procedures, but the counsellor must also remember that he/she alone cannot "be all things to all men".

Freeth (2007) believes the task of mental health professionals is to strive to get the best out of science, while not ever doing this at the expense of relationship, respect and valuing people.

Although this book looks at short-term counselling from both psychodynamic and cognitive–behavioural therapy (CBT) approaches, one thing I stress here and throughout the book is that, in my experience, the relationship between patient and therapist is an important factor in effective counselling. This is well evidenced within the profession of counselling and psychotherapy. Therapist, therapeutic relationship, and non-specific factors are generally found to be more influential ingredients of therapy than are specific therapeutic techniques (Wampold, 2001).

Factors such as therapist's warmth and empathy, and client expectations and willingness to confront problems, are important mediators of change and contribute greatly to the outcome, even within a short-term contract. With only a six-session contact time with a patient, the counsellor does not have the luxury of being precious about his/her particular model. For those uninitiated into the primary care setting, this may seem like an invitation to practise a hotchpotch approach, and I strongly recommend that a trainee on placement only practise within the model they have been taught. However, an experienced counsellor will need to use their skills to mix and match various styles and approaches to tailor-make a six-session contract to fit the patient before them. In other words, the counsellor needs to use a creative approach.

Within the surgery, we find many patients who do not wish to "rely" upon medication, but, although this may seem in their eyes a laudable attitude, some patients will need medication to raise their mood enough to make use of counselling. For many patients, counselling in conjunction with drugs works well. This is endorsed by the Department of Health's booklet *Choosing Talking Therapies* (2002), the research base for which is a Department of Health publication called *Treatment Choice in Psychological Therapies and Counselling: Evidence Based Clinical Guideline* (2001).

I have learnt by experience that the assessment process is the key to effective short-term counselling in primary care as it can help to ensure that *we do not offer what we cannot deliver*.

Finding a common denominator:
what we all share as human beings

It is important that we, as counsellors, never forget that we share with our clients all the problems and vicissitudes of being a part of the human race. When we are distressed and need help and support, we want to be heard as the unique person that we are; a unique person set within unique relationships and environment. Let us not give less to our clients than we need for ourselves.

Physical needs

It almost goes without saying that if a person's basic physical needs are not being met, then distress will occur. If a person's physical needs are not met over a period of time, there will be a lot of distress. These physical needs are:

- oxygen in the air we breathe;
- water;
- nutritious food;
- shelter;
- rest and sleep.

We also need the freedom to stimulate our senses and to exercise our muscles. These physical needs are intimately bound up with our emotional needs. Although, in counselling, we are more concerned with a person's emotional needs, it is always worth checking that all is well physically before assuming a person's distressing symptoms are entirely of an emotional origin.

Emotional needs

- security—a safe environment that allows us to develop fully;
- to be able to receive and give attention;
- a sense of autonomy and control so that we may make choices;
- being emotionally connected to others in terms of friendship and intimacy and to know that at least one other person accepts us for who we are;
- feeling part of and belonging to a wider community;

- a sense of significance and status within social groupings;
- self-esteem borne out of competence and achievement;
- privacy for self-reflection and processing experiences;
- a sense of meaning in our lives and a sense of purpose.

Many people who are referred for counselling in the primary care setting are suffering from unmet basic emotional needs, either on a temporary basis or chronically so. We must understand that we, as counsellors, cannot meet those needs, but we can help facilitate the person recognizing them. We can facilitate exploration in order to help the person move toward a situation where more of their needs can be met, or grieved for if they cannot.

The good news—humans have resources

Along with human needs, we have been equipped with human resources. That is a simple concept to take on board, and yet one little thought about in the general population today. We do not always see ourselves as either the authors of our own lives or that we have what is needed to live those lives in a fulfilling way. We want absolute happiness and absolute control, but we must take on board the concept of compromise. If we can cope with compromise, we can learn to cater for our own need to live individually fulfilling lives, and our desire to be in relationship with others. For our lives to work well enough, we must recognize our need of relationships with other people and, thus, must sometimes put aside some of our individual ambition.

Most of us can, with help, look at and usefully explore what solutions we have successfully found to our problems in the past, and what has thwarted that process. We can look at our habitual ways of thinking and our constructs of the world we live in. With help, we may perhaps see our experiences from different angles in order to live emotionally healthier lives.

Freud (1923b) considered this compromise that humans must make when he saw that the two instincts of self-preservation and sexual instinct have no regard for each other, and so each instinct conflicts with the other. In his topographical model, he gave the social a presence in the psyche, which he called the superego, whose requirements of civilizing and socializing were said to conflict with the desires of the id that were instinctual and pleasure seeking. Thus, the identity of the person, which was felt to be innate and unique, was thought be conflicted in some way by socialization, resulting in the development process being a battle between nature and nurture, both within the individual and between the individual's psyche and society.

One of our tasks in the counselling community is to look at that "battle between nature and nurture" in individual lives (including our own), and to help forge individual ways towards living with this conflict in relative harmony.

Key issues

1. Remember that it is your trust in the power of relationship and in your own relevant intuitions that can, for some people, be the only way to hold on to hope.
2. It is always the patient that holds the key to a helpful outcome, and it is the relationship between counsellor and patient that, as much as anything else, facilitates this and determines how far along the journey to experiencing less distress the patient may manage to get.
3. Thorough assessment is the key to effective short-term counselling.
4. The counsellor must ask him/herself whether they can cope with using a non-directive style of counselling alongside a directive style that fits well within the medical model.
5. We must remember that, in this setting, we are always looking out for, and must listen to, what is true and meaningful for the patient before us.
6. The counsellor must also remember that he/she alone cannot be all things to all men.
7. For a patient to fit exactly into a particular approach would be the ideal rather than the reality.
8. It is important that the trainee in placement only practises the model in which they have been trained
9. Do not offer what you cannot deliver.

CHAPTER ONE

Setting the scene of primary care counselling against the backdrop of a rapidly-evolving NHS service

T his chapter tracks the progress of counselling provision in primary care against the backdrop of the history of the NHS and the rapid changes which have occurred over the last two decades.

We will begin by looking at how changes in the NHS over the past twenty years have affected and continue to have an impact upon the service as we see it today.

Stability and change in the NHS from the late 1940s

Probably most people would agree that the inception of the NHS in the late 1940s was "the best thing since sliced bread", especially in the aftermath of the Second World War, a time when the public purse really was tight. We must never forget those years before the NHS, when even basic healthcare was only for those who could afford it.

What has changed? If the reader is over sixty years of age he/she may remember just how it was and recognize that things have changed out of all recognition. The period from the late 1940s until the late 1980s was a time of relative stability in the NHS, and one could argue that, in that time, it was an improving service. That time of stability can now be seen in stark contrast to the rapid changes that have occurred in the past twenty years.

Until the early 1990s, GP surgeries were accountable to, governed, and funded by Strategic Health Authorities, or FHSAs (Family Health Service Authorities), who were, in turn, accountable to and governed by the NHS.

Beginning of counselling in GP surgeries

Counselling in primary care came on the scene during the 1970s and 1980s, and my colleague and I were privileged to be the first counsellors in Essex to be employed by the FHSA to work in a GP surgery. We were able to negotiate a contract that allowed us to see a limited number of longer-term clients alongside our short-term caseload: short-term being assessment plus six fifty-minute weekly sessions. Compared to most of the counselling in primary care at the present time, this flexibility of contract was a luxury.

It is since the 1980s that counselling in primary care has become popular across the UK. During this time, two organizations were conceived, first the BACP division Counselling in a Medical Setting (now Faculty of Healthcare Counsellors and Psychotherapists, FHCP). Then Counselling in Primary Care (CPC) came along, and the profile and standards of counselling in primary care were enhanced.

Rapid changes in provision of primary care from the 1990s to the present day

The revolutionary move to GP practices managing their own funds and becoming Fund Holders came about in the early 1990s, and this had an impact upon the counselling carried out in primary care. Some surgeries continued to employ counsellors, but other counsellors were eased into being self-employed, and a variety of contracts between GPs and counsellors evolved. No two surgeries had the same working hours, pay, or contract for counsellors. A move towards insisting that the counsellors become self-employed in some areas made sense for the GPs, but, of course, the fallout for the counsellor was loss of sick pay, holiday pay.

At this time the "Primary Care Group" was introduced, where the government directed local GPs to pool their budgets, thus putting an end to financial autonomy within the individual practices. Then, within the next two years, these Primary Care Groups were reorganized into larger units, perhaps up to twenty surgeries, as Primary Care Trusts. The latest move (at the time of going to press) is "GP Clusters", who buy in services. This arrangement is just as it says, GPs clustering together for economic and patient benefit.

In the latest change, the NHS "Agenda for Change" (at the time of going to press), the Primary Care Trusts have been grouped together under the management of Strategic Health Authorities (SHAs), where practices are managed in separate areas similar to those of the old system of the FHSAs. SHAs are responsible for developing strategies for the local health services and ensuring high-quality performance. They manage the NHS locally, and are a key link between the Department of Health and the NHS. They will also ensure that national priorities (such as programmes for improving cancer services) are integrated into local plans. It is proposed that SHAs should merge to cover several counties.

The impact of the above changes upon counselling provision and counsellors working in GP surgeries

The rapid changes over the past twenty years have put counselling and counsellors in primary care in a tenuous position, since they are frequently in the firing line when financial cuts have to be made in order to balance budgets within this part of the NHS. This has brought about insecurity and unrest.

Periods of rapid change highlight areas of difficulty within an organization. Differences between individuals, groups of individuals, assertive behaviour, and a questioning stance are anathema to an evolving organization and can be seen as disruptive and possibly dangerous and something to be eradicated. This can bring about a loss of creativity and sometimes loss of much needed autonomy within staff and sections of the organizational community. This loss is eventually passed on to the patient. Stacey (2003) has observed that when the nature or source of power is changed so that people's dependency needs are challenged and frustrated, they will display general patterns of behaviour that are at the mercy of their infantile unconscious defence mechanisms.

Commissioning

With the NHS moving towards becoming a commissioning service, where there will be commissioning of existing "private" agencies, companies, and individuals (the providers) to provide identified services, counsellors and psychotherapists could become extremely professionally vulnerable. They will be less vulnerable in this new world of NHS commissioning if they learn to think like the commissioners (Watson, 2007).

Know your commissioner

Watson (*ibid.*) sees the responsibility for commissioning psychological therapy services as depending upon the management structure of local services and the local commissioning body, and all are likely to have different structures and decision-making tools for commissioning. Thus, to ensure future employment as a counsellor, you may need to know who currently purchases, or will purchase, your services and whether in the new world of practice-based, locality-based, or city-wide commissioning there is a place for you. You may need to market yourself; in other words, match what you have to offer with the needs of the potential purchasers. That is, in this case, counsellors and therapists matching their services with the needs and demands of the commissioner (NHS).

Practice-based commissioning

Practice-based commissioning is something the reader may have heard of because it is one of the new kids on the block. It is a government policy that devolves responsibility for commissioning services from Primary Care Trusts (PCTs) to local GP practices.

Under practice-based commissioning, practices will be given a commissioning budget, which they will have the responsibility for using in order to provide services. This will involve:

- identifying patient needs;
- designing effective and appropriate health service responses to those needs;
- allocating resources against competing service priorities.

Practice-based commissioning transfers these responsibilities to primary care clinicians (effectively, to local GP practices), with the PCT acting as their agent to procure services.

Regulation

Regulation for psychological therapies is an imminent reality, and the reader would do well to take steps to ensure that they are suitably qualified for future employment in the primary care setting.

The White Paper *Trust Assurance and Safety* (Department of Health, 2007b) announced, "The Government is planning to introduce statutory regulation for applied psychologists, psychotherapists and counsellors and other psychological therapists . . ." (7.2). The body responsible will be the Health Professions Council (HPC), which already regulates thirteen health professions. Work is under way to try to ensure that there is a registration system in place by 2009. This regulation will apply to everyone, wherever they work, and whether they are paid or voluntary.

Currently, all HPC approved qualifications are at degree level. In the past, Regulatory Councils have allowed a period of "grand-parenting", where people already on the registers of Professional Associations can transfer on to the Statutory Register.

Key Issues

1. Counselling provision in primary care has experienced many changes in a short period of time.
2. Thorough assessment, using either a CBT or psychodynamic approach, is key to good outcomes.

3   Know your commissioner. Counsellors are less vulnerable "if they learn to think like the commissioners" (Watson, 2007).

4.   Regulation for psychological therapies is imminent.

CHAPTER TWO

Valuing what you bring to the primary care setting as an experienced or newly graduated counsellor

Containment of anxiety

The ability to contain anxiety is central to counselling work within the primary care setting. The extent to which a person/counsellor can tolerate and contain anxiety is drawn from circumstances of personal growth and development. This is enhanced in the case of the counsellor by an adequate clinical training. This ability to contain anxiety, your own and that of others, does not mean that you will never feel anxious, as anxiety is a normal response to certain situations and part of the human condition.

The perceived and often accepted role of the GP surgery within the community, and, in particular, that of the doctors employed there, is to provide a safe place and foster the belief that within that place there is a knowledge of, and a capacity to cure or control, emotional problems and mental ill health. This perception often has the effect of containing an individual patient's anxiety and often, additionally, their family's anxiety. It may also have the effect of containing the anxiety of surgery staff.

Thus, the ability to recognize your own anxiety and its source is an essential personal tool within the GP surgery. The counsellor may unconsciously be called upon and nominated to contain the anxiety of patients, doctors, and other surgery personnel.

In the medical, caring professions, some professionals take care of their own distress and anxiety by projecting them on to their patients. For example, in a surgery situation, this may result in a doctor or other referring member of staff becoming overwhelmed and emotionally merged or over-identified with his or her patient. This may result in a referral to the counsellor as a matter of urgency when, in fact, there is no urgency. This can put the counsellor under unnecessary strain, and, after the initial assessment, he/she may be left with questions about the actual urgency of the patient's problem.

Example: Dr Peters and Graham

Graham consulted Dr Peters because he had become very anxious over the previous few weeks. Dr Peters quite rightly investigated what had happened recently that might be causing the anxiety. Graham's wife had asked for a divorce and his eldest daughter had just gone to university. A similar situation had happened to Dr Peters in the past, as a result of which he had experienced feelings and thoughts about suicide. Consequently, Dr Peters over-reacted to Graham's anxiety and referred him for an urgent assessment with the counsellor.

* * *

There may also be issues around meeting targets within the primary care team, for example, cutting down on expensive medication or containing tier two mental illness within primary care (that is, illness that is normally considered more suitably contained by inpatient care and/or outpatient care under a psychiatrist). These can raise the anxiety levels of some or all staff, including the surgery counsellor.

Knowledge of unconscious processes

This book makes the assumption that counsellors trained to diploma level in whatever discipline of counselling will have a working knowledge of unconscious processes and be aware of the power these processes can exert in the patient, the counsellor, and the supervisor. Later, this text widens our knowledge of unconscious processes to include organizations including especially the medical organization of the primary care setting. This knowledge is one of the greatest assets a counsellor can take into their working life within the primary care setting.

Attachment style

Counsellors are (or should be) familiar with their own attachment style, and are, therefore, in a good position to empathize with the patient on the one hand, and yet able to maintain strong boundaries on the other. Patients with different attachment patterns often benefit from different models of counselling. The counsellor who has the ability to assess his or her patient's attachment style, inner-world dynamics, and prevailing thought and behaviour patterns will be able to offer help from either a CBT or a psychodynamic approach.

Experience of the aetiology of psychopathology and personality

As with the above, counsellors trained to diploma level will have a good grounding in the aetiology of certain thought patterns, behaviours, mental illness, mental distress, and mental disorders. I take as axiomatic that all counsellors in training to diploma level will have included at least one year of clinical training, supervision, and personal therapy.

The counsellor's ability to act as mediator within the primary care team

In staff conflict caused by situations where, for instance, it is unclear who holds the medical responsibility for a certain patient or decision, and that is clearly exacerbated by the staff members' personal past "baggage", the counsellor can offer the service of tactful and delicate mediation.

Example: Joyce and Joan

A health visitor and practice nurse who had worked alongside each other relatively harmoniously for many years came into conflict over a certain vulnerable, young lady patient. Each one felt they held responsibility for this person's health and emotional well-being, and the situation became heated. Joyce, the health visitor, approached the surgery counsellor for help. The counsellor agreed to a one-off session with Joyce, which uncovered much harbouring of ill feeling by her towards Joan, the practice nurse. This had accrued over many years and had come to a head over the young lady.

It transpired that Joyce had grown up the eldest girl of a large family and, consequently, had taken a large amount of responsibility within the home with childcare and cooking. She found a significance in this, but secretly harboured resentment at not being free to play and, in adolescence, to go out dancing. What we uncovered in our session was how she felt the practice nurse was stealing her "significance", and had done so, as she felt, many times before within the team. It was a painful but honest session, where Joyce felt heard and understood and was able to see how her past conflict was colouring the present situation. Subsequently, she was able to be more objective.

Acquaintance with the darker side: socially structured defence mechanisms

The GP surgery setting that provides containment for anxiety also has a darker side; it may, at times, defend against the anxiety that can stem from the urgency and immediacy of patient and surgery staff needs. It is important that the counsellor is able to recognize these widely held, socially structured defence mechanisms. These mechanisms can be very powerful, and can operate in such a way as to promote the unconscious defence mechanisms of denial, projection, splitting, medicalization, and somatization among patients, members of surgery staff, counsellors, and their supervisors.

Menzies (1984) considers that the kinds of problems and situations that are everyday occurrences within medical helping agencies unconsciously stimulate afresh in practitioners their own early situations and their accompanying emotions. This may put a person at risk of being flooded by intense and unmanageable anxiety. One important aspect of these socially structured defence mechanisms is an attempt by individuals to externalize and give objective reality to their particular psychic defence mechanism. What then happens over time, as the result of unconscious collusion between the staff, is that a social defence system occurs, the form of which the members have unconsciously agreed. In other words, this social defence system then tends to become the external reality. In the GP surgery, this is evident in the culture, ethos, and prevailing belief and value system, which shows itself as medicalization, somatization, control, hierarchy, splitting, and, often, collusion in the denial and hiding of psychic pain. It can be so pervasive that counsellors and supervisors can become caught up in this collusion.

Menzies (*ibid.*) believes the characteristic feature of the social defence system is its orientation to helping the individuals involved to avoid the experience of anxiety, doubt, uncertainty, and guilt. This avoidance can never be fully successful, and a compromise is inevitable between the implicit aims of the social defence system and the person's real emotional needs. The system's defences are typical of the young infant's attempts to deal with, mainly by evasion, the intense anxieties aroused by the interplay of his own instincts that are intolerable at his immature age (Bion, 2002).

Patients who are regressed, for example, because of bereavement, abandonment, or in some other way vulnerable and dependent, may come up against a system that does nothing to confront or understand those primitive defence mechanisms. Often, the content of their fantasy anxiety situations is not brought into effective contact with reality until they consult with an experienced counsellor within the medical setting.

What constitutes health gain: the distinction between social adjustment and cure of the soul

Fromm (1977) makes the distinction in psychoanalysis between the "social adjustment" and the "cure of the soul". It has often been my experience that the unconscious agenda of the GP is towards social adjustment (often under pressure from the patient and/or the patient's family), rather than cure of the soul. The psychodynamic counsellor's training would encourage him/her towards "cure of the soul", but this often comes up against the unconscious pressure of social adjustment, and collusion or collision can occur. The CBT counsellor may or may not be aware of this collision, since their model fits better with the medical model of the primary care setting. The present government's focus on evidence-based medicine adds extra pressure upon the primary care counsellor to prove that counselling is effective. There is some disagreement about what constitutes health gain. It could be argued that one of the reasons that CBT sits well within the medical model is that often, after this treatment, there can be seen the disappearance of symptoms or the subjugation of behaviours. Mearns (1998), who is trained in person-centred counselling, moots that counselling merely gives social gains and not always health gains.

Knowledge and importance of boundaries within the primary care setting

In the counselling and psychotherapy world, the word "boundary" takes on an additional meaning to that which society may normally mean by it. The *Concise Oxford Dictionary* sums it up well: "Boundary—a line marking the limits of an area". In addition to the physical boundary, that is, the actual counselling room, there are specific unseen boundaries in the primary care setting that must be adhered to. These unseen boundaries are importantly kept in any counselling setting where counselling is the main function of a building. In these settings, the occupants share the respect of the normal contracted boundaries. However, although in the primary care setting of the GP surgery or health centre boundaries are also kept with similar respect, the counsellor may experience these boundaries as sometimes unhelpfully different to those of private counselling practice or a counselling agency centre. It is sometimes harder in the primary care setting to hold the boundaries of place, time, and confidentiality. However, a counsellor's observance of the rule of abstinence and respect for race, culture, faith, and difference is normally in accordance with those of the rest of the primary care team.

In this text, I call the appropriate set of counselling boundaries the "frame". The tight, non-permeable frame that I believed I had practised as a counsellor in an agency and in private practice up until my employment as a counsellor in a GP surgery needed to be rethought. Langs speaks of the frame of counselling and psychotherapy as being the "setting and ground rules . . . unique set of conditions that distinguish and frame a psychotherapeutic experience" (Langs, 1993, p. 4). Although this reference speaks of psychotherapy, counselling pays as much attention to frame issues as does the practice of psychotherapy, whether in a surgery or another setting. Langs (*ibid.*) considers that no frame is totally secure and that all therapy operates within a "deviant" frame. Although Langs suggests that it is usually the patient who puts pressure upon the counsellor to deviate from the tight frame, he has also found that, through encoded verbal communication, the patient will ask for the frame to remain as secure as possible in order to gain the benefit of what Langs call the "special therapeutic opportunity of the secure-frame moment" (Langs, 1988, p. 148).

The surgery is a much more porous atmosphere than private practice, and the counsellor needs to be aware of forces from many different directions that can have an impact upon his/her work and ability to hold boundaries. These could be increasing numbers and sources of referral, administration time (often time not valued by payment), creating a private space in which to work (a consistent space with noise and interruptions kept to a minimum), and differing staff and patient expectations. These can all put huge pressure upon the counsellor.

Variables within the primary care setting that may put the secure frame under threat

A different concept of confidentiality

This is an area where understanding of the concept of confidentiality by a GP or other primary care staff may vary from the counsellor's. The doctor or member of staff may want, and attempt, to elicit from the counsellor information about counselling content. He/she may also ask the counsellor to see another member of the patient's family. The notion of confidentiality within the primary care setting is often that all information about patients is confidential to the primary care setting rather than to one individual member of staff. This may seem anathema to a newly employed counsellor, and can cause him/her conflict as he/she wishes to be accepted and seen to co-operate with other staff members on the one hand, but wishes to remain faithful to his/her ethical framework on the other hand. However, I have found that once the reasons for a much tighter control of confidentiality are explained to staff, they respect the reasons, even if they do not fully understand how it can help the therapeutic experience.

I have found that it is often the receptionists who find it most difficult to empathize or identify with a patient who wishes, as far as possible in this setting, to remain anonymous within the waiting and reception areas. I am also aware that, for the newly employed or trainee placement counsellor, receptionists can some-times seem rather fierce and to have considerable power. With all due respect to receptionists, I have also often found them to be most helpful and, in my opinion, they are definitely the unsung heroes of the primary care setting, as they have to deal with some very difficult and testing situations, both on the telephone and at reception.

Inappropriate information giving

A GP or other referring member of staff (health visitor, practice nurse) may give the counsellor information that is unhelpful for him/her to have before the patient him/herself is ready to reveal it. The member of staff usually believes they are being helpful, as they may not fully understand the nature of counselling. Again, an explanation given in a sensitive way is usually all it takes to gain co-operation in this area.

Example: information given in the doctor's referral letter

Dr John wrote in his referral letter to the counsellor that a gang of young homosexual men had anally raped his patient Gavin, a young man of nineteen. This incident, traumatizing in itself, had brought back memories of when he was raped as a child and the accompanying fear and shame he had felt when his parents informed the police. When Gavin came for his assessment and for the next two sessions, although wanting to talk about the recent rape, he was finding it impossible to disclose to the counsellor about the childhood rape. The counsellor, having been given the facts of the childhood rape from the GP and feeling pressured by the short-term contract, found it difficult to allow Gavin to disclose the abuse how and when he needed to.

The boundaries of time and place

The medical model of place and time often differs from those thought to facilitate therapeutic counselling outcomes. GPs usually have their own designated consulting room, which they consider "belongs" to them. Some surgeries and health centres have a designated counselling room, or at least a room that is not a doctor's consulting room. Unfortunately, the latter can be used for other purposes, and it has been my experience that counsellors sometimes have to "fight" for their space. It is usually a good plan to "make friends" with the practice manager, who is often in charge of allocating rooms.

A problematic situation can occur when counselling happens in a GP's consulting room on his/her day off. This arrangement usually works without hitch, but sometimes GPs change their days off without informing either the counsellor or the practice manger, and a counsellor can find him/herself in the difficult situation of having nowhere to see the patient. The worst-case scenarios that I have experienced are conducting the counselling in the staff room, small treatment room, or even the kitchen! These situations call upon the counsellor's assertiveness skills, resilience, and ability to be flexible.

Take heart, for even when times and rooms are changed against our better judgement, it is amazing how a patient seems hardly to notice, and, although this may temporarily faze the counsellor, as long as he/she keeps calm and containing, the patient invariably makes the best of what is being offered, despite the strange surroundings.

As you may observe from the above, the surgery setting is a much more porous atmosphere than private practice, but I believe that once a counsellor becomes aware of the differences and anomalies he/she can adapt and work within the constraints and still reap the rewards of working within a team. East (1995) says "counsellors must walk the tightrope of being collaborative and communicative, while rigorously maintaining the overriding ethic of confidentiality for their clients" (p. 131).

Holding the "unholdable"

It is often the counsellor in a GP surgery who is unconsciously allocated the difficult task of holding the "unholdable". This phenomenon of mentally and emotionally holding the tensions and paradoxes that arise within the primary care team due to differing ideas, perceptions and expectations occurs at an unconscious level. Because of this, it does mean that the counsellor must be ever vigilant and must ask him/herself certain questions as proposed by Coe (2008), in order to maintain an ethical and therapeutic stance. He asks:

- Is there a clear reason for this boundary-crossing action based on my client's need?

- Does my behaviour towards this client differ from my behaviour towards other clients?

- Am I reluctant to discuss some things about my work with this client with my supervisor?

- Am I working beyond my training?

- Am I concerned about how my client may be experiencing my actions?

- Am I checking that my actions are for my client's benefit?

- What will my action mean to the client?

- What might the effects be?

- Might the client feel "special", different from other clients?

- Will the relationship remain clearly a professional one, or might it become ambiguous and uncertain? [ibid., p. 14]

The impact on the frame of broken or insecure boundaries

As with the above section, I deal here with the impact of broken or insecure boundaries in terms of the security of time, place, and confidentiality. I take as a given the suggestion I made earlier that although the setting is more porous than private practice, it is still the responsibility of the primary care counsellor to hold the frame for the patient as securely as possible.

The impact of time breaks

By time breaks, I refer to changes to the day of the week, the time of day, and other breaks in the continuity of counselling. As you will have observed in your own personal position as a patient in a GP surgery, continuity of time can be a relaxed affair. In fact, the act of waiting and the changing of times is often the norm. With change and transition of any kind there always comes a sense of loss, and it is important that a counsellor acknowledges that sense of loss not only in their clients but also in him/herself.

The whole spectrum of emotion that is activated by loss comes into play, whether acknowledged or unacknowledged. By considering afresh the stages of loss and grief, its impact can be monitored carefully in order for it to be used in the counselling process. The counsellor must also be aware of his/her own inner processing.

An obvious impact on the patient of the surgery (in the patient's mind, the counsellor) changing time or day is that it gives the unconscious message that they, too, have permission to change times, cancel, and act out in unhelpful ways. Unfortunately, in some primary care settings, the impact of the above has to be lived with and can become grist to the mill for the surgery counsellor: everything can be worked with providing the patient actually arrives for his/her counselling session.

Example: Paul

Paul, who had been referred for counselling after the death of his father, attended regularly and on time until the counsellor was forced to change his appointment time due to a chaotic room situation on a particular day. The next week, he telephoned to ask if the counsellor could see him on a different day and at a different time, because it would fit in better with his work shift pattern. Now, although this seems a reasonable request, it is unlikely that Paul would have made it if the counsellor had been able to maintain continuity of day and time for the whole of the patient's contract.

The impact of change of place

Within the primary care setting, by change of place I refer to change of room. I have already intimated above how this scenario can occur due to the nature of the allocating of rooms. It is often a luxury for a primary care counsellor to have a room of his or her own. The room may be designated as the counselling room, but, when needs must, it will be used for other purposes, such as weighing babies or the visit of a consultant. Counselling is rarely deemed to be the most important function in the surgery. It is, therefore, very important for the counsellor to recognize the impact of a change of room, both on the patient and on themselves. At an unconscious level, we are no more resilient in the face of change than our clients. What we have to our advantage is the knowledge and understanding of the impact of change. Sometimes the counsellor's reaction to change is not uncovered until the patient and their material is taken to supervision. Supervision is something I will speak more about later in this book.

The impact of breaks in confidentiality

Breaks in confidentiality refer to times when client material leaks out from the frame of the counselling arena. I include the counsellor's consultation with his/her supervisor as being held within the arena of the frame.

It is my experience that the patient often has an unspoken expectation that people within the primary care setting may discuss their "case" medically. For example, a nurse may speak to a doctor, or a doctor may speak to a consultant, about a patient's case. This has been accepted as a medical norm. So, a patient may extrapolate from this that a counsellor may speak to another member of the primary care team about his/her situation or symptoms. There may also be an expectation among primary care staff, before the coun-sellor has educated them to the contrary, that he/she may do like-wise. It may also apply in the opposite direction: for example, a doctor or another member of the primary care team may compro-mise the counsellor and patient relationship by sharing information which is not helpful to the therapeutic experience. Doctors may also suggest that the counsellor consult a patient's medical records if required. Many counsellors feel uncomfortable with this.

I have found, however, that there will be instances where the counsellor will need to have certain information about the patient before he/she arrives for counselling. The nature and extent of this information needs to be negotiated with the primary care team. For example, it is useful for the counsellor to know if a person has just made a suicide attempt, has had a recent stay in a psychiatric hospi-tal, or wishes to discuss a possible termination of pregnancy. I say this as it has been my experience that the patient will automatically assume that the counsellor will have this knowledge and may not think to tell the counsellor of this or something similarly urgent or important. It could be argued that it is up to the patient to inform the counsellor of what they wish them to know, and in other coun-selling settings I would agree with this, but it is the short-term nature of the counselling that is on offer at the surgery that makes it necessary for this boundary to be occasionally broken.

Example of an unhelpful scenario

The counsellor, not having yet met the patient, is greeted by the receptionist saying something like, "Oh you're seeing Mrs Smith, well, she's always up here making a fuss and trying to see the doctor—you've got your hands full there."

Before you think that this could never happen, know that the example that I have just given was a real one with exception of the name of the patient! Take this as a salutary example and give your-self some time to think about how that exchange with the recep-tionist could influence the way in which you, the counsellor, may approach the patient in question. It does not take a huge leap of the imagination to see how the above could compromise the beginning of the counselling arrangement, and also how the receptionist may not see her contribution as a breach of confidentiality.

There is not room here to give an exhaustive list of the ways in which confidentiality could be breached almost inadvertently but I do want to add a word of caution regarding the counsellor contacting the patient to set up the first counselling contact. This note of caution also applies to when it might be necessary to contact the patient during the duration of that contract. Another member of the patient's family or household could answer the telephone, and it is important to hold the boundaries of confidentiality very firmly in this instance.

There will also be instances when the counsellor needs to speak to a GP for reasons of safety for the patient. It is always advisable, where possible, to do this with the patient's knowledge and after discussion with him/her about why this needs to happen and how they feel about it. Sometimes, a patient asks you to speak to a GP on their behalf for various reasons. Again, discussion about this with the patient is essential, as you may both come to the conclusion that a better course of action would be for the patient to see the GP first and then come to talk over the result with the counsellor afterwards.

As in any other counselling situation, our ultimate aim is a move towards increased autonomy for the patient and not greater dependency. However, it is widely recognized that, with longer-term counselling, dependency may be a necessary step towards ultimate growth in autonomy.

The possibility of notes being subpoenaed by the courts

It is advisable to keep only basic, factual counselling information on patients in the surgery building, for example, name, address, and dates of attendance. The reader should familiarize themselves with the law regarding subpoenaing of notes, as this is also a break of confidentiality that must be thought about. The notes of counselling being carried out in primary care are more likely to be subpoenaed than in private practice. Solicitors do not hesitate to contact a person's GP for information, and this may spill over into the counselling domain. This can be worrying and intimidating for the counsellor, especially, due to the intense and immediate stress and distress of their patient when a court appearance is imminent. This immediate stress is likely to find its way to the GP in the first instance and, subsequently, to the surgery counsellor.

When starting work in the primary care setting, the practice manager may inform the counsellor how and where to store their notes. If this does not happen, the counsellor should consider, perhaps in consultation with their supervisor or mentor, the best way to record and store notes in order to minimize breaches of confidentiality (a) in the building itself, and (b) for the possible subpoenaing of counsellor's notes. Help on this topic can be obtained from the appropriate BACP Information Sheet.

Ways that a client may try to break boundaries in the GP surgery setting

What I am speaking of here is not the obvious ways, such as, for instance, the patient asking whether their spouse/parent can attend the next session, or asking you straight questions about your own life, but the more subtle ways in which it may occur. The patient may unconsciously attempt to set up a rivalry situation between you and the GP. He or she may try to play one off against the other by "spilling out" material in both consultation arenas and perhaps intimating that one practitioner is "better" than the other. This can be quite seductive for both counsellor and GP, and this unconscious sabotage needs to be addressed as soon as possible. Always bear in mind that inside a "manipulative" patient hides an inner child who has not been appropriately heard and taken seriously. When there are several primary care personnel involved with a patient simultaneously, subtle boundary breaking is much more likely to occur.

The distinction between the processes of short-term and longer-term counselling

As a psychodynamic counsellor or CBT therapist, your main training to diploma level will almost certainly have been in practising longer-term counselling. CBT therapists will have been trained to work also with a shorter-term model, but probably not as short-term as the assessment plus six-session model often practised in the primary care setting. Thus, you will have knowledge of the process of long-term counselling and therapy. In long-term work, you will be familiar with looking at the bigger picture, both assessing how the therapeutic relationship has developed over time, and also what mutative experience the client has had, or resisted having, mentally, behaviourally, emotionally, and developmentally. You will also be familiar with your personal position of subjective objectivity, that is, being part of the drama being played out in the counselling arena. You will be able, with the help of supervision, to analyse and conceptualize that drama, and your part in it, from a safe and objective distance. Obviously, the main difference in the processes of longer-term and short-term work is time itself.

Time: a strange phenomenon

Time is a funny thing. Although we experience time as linear with our clocks, timetables, and seasons, our inner world or unconscious mind, does not experience it that way. The relatively new discipline of neuroscience is currently shedding more light upon the chemical and organic workings of our minds.

Gefter, in an article titled "Time's up" (2008), speaks of time as the invisible presence that governs our world.

> Trailing you like an unshakeable shadow, it ticks and tocks incessantly—you can sense it in your heartbeat, in the rising and setting of the sun, and in your daily rush to make meetings, trains and deadlines. It brings order to our lives through the categories of past, present and future. [p. 26]

Gefter then goes on to tell us that the passage of time is not absolute, that time differs from one frame of reference to the next.

We see this anomaly in our understanding and experience of time played out very clearly with the phenomenon of post traumatic stress disorder (PTSD), where a person can experience the trauma of the past as if it were happening in the present. In a happier and more creative way, we can experience the "past in the present" when, for instance, we smell newly mown grass and realize how that sensation is evocative of our childhood.

Let us expand upon what was said about time not being experienced as linear in the unconscious mind. It is through this unique phenomenon that it is possible to observe the macrocosm of transference of longer-term counselling working in the microcosm of the short-term contract. The two big differences between the processes of longer-term and short-term counselling are our attitude to time, and to how we deal with the transference experience.

The "time" experience of how many sessions the patient has at his or her disposal, and how many are left in the contract, can be explored and discussed in each session. This can have the effect of heightening the transference and causing anxiety. In longer-term counselling, this anxiety would generally not be overtly noted between counsellor and patient, but would be used by the counsellor to explore the person's inner world through the transference relationship. However, with short-term counselling, the counsellor does not have the "luxury" of doing this and must help the person, in the here and now, to see what is happening. For instance, making a comment to the patient, something like, "You seem to be responding to me as if I am your mother/father" can help them to gain insight. Having brought this out into the arena of the session, the counsellor may be able to help the patient towards understanding his relationships, both to others and to himself or herself.

So, let us look at the process of short-term counselling, which is assessment plus six fifty-minute sessions. In this truncated version of counselling, we still importantly have a beginning, middle, and an end. In my experience it is the beginning—the assessment—that is the most important event, as it is here that we assess whether the person can make use of short-term counselling effectively. The assessment of a person and their psychopathology is worth spending a substantial amount of time on with the patient. If it cannot be completed in an hour and a half, it is useful to use the first session of the six-week contract to complete it and to find a focus for the work. The reader will need processing time to look at his/her inner response to the person, and to make a hypothetical treatment plan. I say hypothetical, as patients love to prove us wrong. We must always endeavour to be flexible in our hypotheses and our thinking. It may also be necessary to take that assessment to supervision if you feel you have an unhelpful identification with the patient, or if their presenting problem is out of your experience thus far in your working life. I deal with assessments in full later in the text.

Manifest and hidden agenda

When a patient presents himself or herself for short-term counselling, there is always a manifest agenda and a hidden agenda, both for the therapist and the patient. The patient will have a transference relationship with the therapist whether he/she is of psychodynamic orientation or CBT trained. This may be a complicated transference, as it will be contaminated by the patient's transference to the referring doctor, nurse, or other member of staff. This is a lot for the patient to contend with, as the feelings he/she has about the surgery environment will also be transferred to the counsellor, who, for them, is part of the surgery.

Your personal experience of a GP surgery

Although I mention this last on the list of what you bring to the setting, it is by no means the least of what you bring. You will almost certainly have been a patient in a GP surgery for some, if not all, of your life if you have lived in the UK. The experience of being a patient encompasses your experience of transference (positive and negative) and countertransference to the GPs and other surgery personnel. The reader also brings concrete and practical experience.

What the counsellor stands to gain from employment as a counsellor in a GP surgery

Most counsellors who have been employed to counsel in the primary care setting, and trainee counsellors in their clinical placement, have found it a rewarding experience. In addition, they are able to further their careers with invaluable experience of the whole spectrum of human distress and mental ill health. The reader has the opportunity to gain experience in recognizing and understanding the wide variety of neuroses and psychoses. Nothing can compare with the experience of relationships with patients who show you in their behaviour and psychopathology that which, up until now, you may only have learnt about in textbooks. In other words, it is the practice of the work that puts flesh on the theory. You embark upon a steep learning curve when you begin this important work.

The counsellor will also experience and begin to understand organizational dynamics and their impact on counselling and supervision, surgery personnel and patients. The primary care setting is made up of individual people interacting with each other, and it is these interactions that determine how people act and react individually, as part of a group or as part of a sub-group. For instance, the pharmacists are a sub-group, as are the receptionists. This can be tough, as it is sometimes difficult to remain objective while working and "living" in the setting. It may be during supervision that these dynamics can be seen more clearly, and also their impact. However, it must always be borne in mind that your supervisor will be, or have been, a patient in primary care him/herself, and is, thus, prey to the same unconscious processes regarding that setting as you are. It is helpful to the work if this is made explicit between you.

Another gain is, that as a counsellor in primary care, this may be your first paid employment as a counsellor and, as there is never a shortage of patients, this could be your first secure, long-term employment. This can be a useful validating and affirming experience, as you could well have worked until now as a voluntary or trainee counsellor.

Key issues

1. The ability to contain anxiety is central to counselling work within the primary care setting.
2. The GP surgery setting that provides containment for anxiety also has a darker side—a socially structured defence mechanism.
3. Know your own attachment style and assess the patient's.
4. Be aware of the difference between cure of the soul and social adjustment.
5. It is sometimes harder in the primary care setting to hold the boundaries of place, time and confidentiality.
6. In a clinical medical setting there is a different concept of confidentiality.
7. It is often the counsellor in a GP surgery who is unconsciously allocated the difficult task of holding the "unholdable".

CHAPTER THREE

Introduction and induction into the GP surgery

When first being employed or entering a placement in a GP surgery, the counsellor may need to take proactive steps to elicit the services of the lead GP or the practice manager to carry out a formal introduction to the staff and to the workings of both the building and the organizational running of the practice. Knowing how everything works and knowing who to ask for help and information can go a long way towards helping the counsellor feel confident and informed from the beginning. For instance, in some surgeries, there may be a separate waiting area for counselling, or the counselling room may be in an area quite separate from the general workings of the surgery. In this instance, the counsellor may have very little contact with the receptionists, and consequently they may not know who you are when a patient asks to see you. This is easily remedied with a little effort from the counsellor. You may or may not have access to a computer that is linked to other computers in the surgery, and it may be by computer screen that you will be alerted when your patient arrives.

The explicit and implicit organizational dynamics of the primary care setting

Hawkins and Shohet (2000) define organizational culture as the different explicit and implicit assumptions and values that influence the behaviour and social artefacts of different groups. It is well to remember, as put forward by Morgan (1986), that the organization does not exist in a vacuum; it is part of, and related to, the environment, which comprises a number of interrelated sub-systems, and also, that to flourish, there needs to be an internal congruency between the sub-systems.

Counsellors must remember that they are subject to the same group pressures as everyone else; they are competitive, resistant, and reluctant to expose their failures, weaknesses, incompetence, and insecurities.

Explicit clues

Explicit clues about organizational dynamics of the setting can be gathered during the counsellor's introduction to the staff in the surgery, and induction into the workings of that unique setting.

What to look for

How you are introduced to the members of surgery staff can give a clue to the "traditions" that take place there; for instance, the manner in which people like to be referred to, such as by their first names or more formally. When these introductions happen, they can give a clue to the importance placed upon your comfort and successful integration into the staff team. As a new member of staff, the counsellor may be invited to the GPs' weekly meeting, where you will have an opportunity to say something about yourself and how you would like to work in the surgery. At this meeting, you will be able to observe how the partners address each other and whether there is an obvious hierarchy.

It will also become clear whether it is the lead GP or the practice manager who "wears the trousers" in the day-to-day running of the surgery. However, whatever seems obvious to you at this time, it is a fact that the practice manager has a good deal of power.

Some managers like to wield this power, but others take a more democratic stance.

If you are able to be introduced early on to all members of staff, it is likely that you will feel less of an "add on" to the staff team and, thus, feel more valued from the beginning.

The actual counselling room that you are allocated for your work gives another clue to what and who is valued in that setting. As I mentioned earlier, there is not always a designated counselling room, which means that a nurse's or GP's consulting room will double up as a counselling room. The situation regarding rooms will be become obvious to you at your induction, and it can be telling, when you ask questions about the availability of the room, whether your work and its boundaries will be respected and valued. It may be not until there are monetary restraints put upon the primary care practice that one's value (or the value of counselling) is truly seen. When there is an overspend, counselling may be one of the first services under review for cuts, as it is sometimes regarded as an optional extra. This can be the case even though GPs know what patients need, as they may be overruled by the PCT.

Implicit clues

Implicit clues are gleaned as you personally experience the unique dynamics of the setting. Stacey (2003) suggests that the individual mind can be thought of as a system made up of interacting concepts, and a group may be thought of as a system consisting of interacting individuals. This idea can give us a good indication of just how complicated the "unconscious system" may be that is operating within the primary care team. I propose that staff within a GP surgery or health centre take on and absorb the cultural influences of the primary care setting. Consequently, individuals can be seen to operate differently inside the surgery from outside in the community. For example, there may be some institutionally sanctioned breaking of boundaries within the setting, such as gossip within the staffroom, or there may be group and sub-group behaviour that the individuals concerned would not be seen engaging in outside of the setting. Also, the new counsellor may accommodate some breaking of confidentiality or time boundaries in order to be welcome within the surgery "family" and to be accepted by the GPs, to whom he/she may have a childlike transference.

The implicit balance of power

The balance of power within the setting is another issue that can impose subtle pressures upon the dynamics between individuals, groups, and sub-groups. Dalal (2001) puts forward that it is power that patterns the "communicational field" (Foulkes, 1990), where communications are likely to flow more in certain directions and less in others.

When a new counsellor or other member of staff is first taken on by the GP practice, it is he/she who is in the position of being the "not we" in relation to the "we" of the established surgery group (doctors, pharmacists, nurses, and receptionists, etc.) (Dalal, 2001). It is the greater cohesion of the "we" who have the upper hand in the power differential in relation to the "not we". The above unique "mix", or, as I prefer to call it, "dance", can lead to some individuals or groups within the primary care setting feeling isolated, frustrated, and powerless. These feelings can lead to passive aggression, which may be acted out in certain unconscious ways: for instance, lack of co-operation, poor communication, and ill health among the staff.

Induction

At his/her induction, the counsellor must be ready to take some responsibility for gleaning what they feel they need to know about procedures, protocols, surgery opening times, etc.

It is important for the new counsellor to consider what he/she will need to know from their induction into GP surgery practice. The first of these being, of course, who will carry out the induction. He/she will need to know the system for receiving and recording messages from patients, and how and when those messages will be passed on. The new counsellor may decide upon a system that suits them and ask the receptionist to implement it. Some surgeries have a computer in the counselling room and all necessary information will come up on the screen. You will also need to know how reception will alert you to a client waiting (if not via the computer screen) and how you will receive them into the counselling room: will the receptionist point the way or will you go to the waiting area to collect the patient?

Typical day in the life of a primary care counsellor in a GP surgery or health centre

This section takes the reader through a variety of possible events taking place on a typical day in the surgery and an opportunity to reflect upon his/her emotional reactions to them.

A typical day

You enter the car park, where you may meet your first patient getting out of their car. You walk in and greet the receptionists, who may say something like, "Oh, Val, your Mrs Smith isn't coming, she'll see you next week." This can be very annoying, especially if the receptionist took the message the evening before and could have telephoned to inform you in good time for you to fill the space.

You look in your pigeonhole or tray for messages and find a scrap of paper saying, "Can we meet asap to talk about Mrs Smith, John."

Then, you go into the counselling room, which may be a doctor's consulting room, prepare it, which may include clearing a space on the desk (including unmentionables like used throat spatulas or KY jelly!), putting on the heater, and opening the curtains.

The phone rings; it is the receptionist, who says, "Your new lady is here. She's got her husband with her!" (This is said with great feeling and emphasis in which you can hear her nod and wink.)

You go to the waiting room to collect client (and husband). You recognize another client in the waiting room and immediately panic, thinking you have double booked. But no, she just gives you a cheery wave.

You deal with the "husband situation" in the counselling room. He wants to know if you are good enough to see his wife. He stays, and after fifteen minutes you ask him whether he feels ready to leave his wife with you. He leaves, and you carry out the assessment. The client leaves and you are able to write some quick notes to be completed later.

You go to the waiting room for your next client. Dr John is just coming out of his consulting room and catches you unawares. "Have you got a sec?" You think, "Yes, I've got a sec, but that's not what you really want!" You look at your watch hoping he'll get the message, but no, because doctors do not work to time boundaries. You manage to arrange a time to meet him later in the day.

After the next client, you grab a coffee and try to find Dr John, as arranged, but one of the receptionists informs you that he has gone out on a call.

Another receptionist asks, "Did you see Dr John, he was looking for you?" You reply, "No, but I should be seeing him now." The receptionist, shaking her head, replies defensively, "Oh dear, it's very urgent." You then feel a bit guilty (or angry) because the receptionist is a personal friend of the doctor and has been in the surgery since the year dot and is very protective of Dr John.

You drink your coffee, which is now lukewarm, and then collect your next client from the waiting room.

In middle of this counselling session, the phone rings again. It is the receptionist telling you that Dr John is back, and then, responding to your silence, she says, "Oh, sorry, I didn't know you had a patient with you."

It is now lunchtime and Dr John is eating his sandwiches (the ones his wife drops off every day in a little basket with a freshly laundered napkin [envy]). You are really hungry by now, but you stay and listen to Dr John. You contain his anxiety about his suicidal patient and promise to fit the patient in at 4 p.m. that day.

Your reactions to the above and other breaching of boundaries

Think about how you would like to handle a situation where you meet a client outside of the surgery, for example, in the car park, in a shop, or in the street. Try to imagine how this may make you feel and how you might handle it with sensitivity and tact.

You will almost certainly be unaccustomed, in a non-primary care setting, to receiving messages about and from patients (perhaps naming the patient) that may be left in your tray or pigeonhole without the privacy of an envelope. This cavalier way of treating patient information may make you feel angry and is never easy to become accustomed to in primary care. This does not occur in every primary care setting.

It is essential that the new counsellor be prepared to be flexible and ready for the possibility of counselling in less than ideal conditions. Obviously, the best scenario is that there is a designated counselling room, but counsellors have worked in a kitchen, staff room, and even a large cupboard. When you find yourself shown to a GP's consulting room, you may have to supply your own clock and tissues, clear away certain items from the surfaces, and use the chairs that are normally used for the GP's consultations, which are more suited to medical problems.

The above examples drawn from "A typical day", above, show the possible difficult situations that may arise, or, at least, ones that are out of the norm for most counselling settings. The whole spectrum of emotions can be evoked, especially when a situation happens for the first time. These emotions can range from panic to embarrassment, anger, and fear. You will need to become an expert in setting firm boundaries. Be prepared also to feel great compassion in the presence of some patients and surprise in the presence of others. In some rare instances, you may experience shock and possibly be traumatized by what you hear.

Key issues

1. Counsellors must remember they are subject to the same group pressures as everyone else. They are competitive, resistant, and reluctant to expose their failures, weaknesses, incompetencies, and insecurities.

CHAPTER FOUR

Finding your place in the medical organizational "family"

The primary care setting can be viewed as a "family", comprising all the family dynamics and systems normally found in an extended family (Reeves, 1998).

This section gives the reader guidance in reflecting upon how their experience of their family of origin can influence how well they begin to find their feet in the surgery. For example, think about whether your family of origin was a patriarchal or a matriarchal family. What was your position in the family, and where were you in the pecking order? Did you feel heard and significant? Was anger expressed actively or passively? In order to make sense of some of your responses and reactions within the primary care setting, it is worth spending time thinking about the above in some depth.

Also remember that the "history" of the organizational setting of the surgery "family" will affect your arrival as a new counsellor. You will be walking on to the stage of a drama that is under way and where all the cast have their roles in place (Dalal, 2001).

It is also worth taking some time to gain an awareness of the multiple transferences, countertransferences, and roles within the surgery, including your own. The CBT therapist will have an opportunity to observe behaviours within the "family" and surmise what thought patterns and feelings may underlie them.

When the counselling takes place in a building separate from the surgery

Sometimes, GP surgeries share a counsellor or counsellors who work in a separate building, perhaps a family centre or a clinic. There will be different dynamics and systems in this setting.

One counsellor whom I supervised described the place in which she counselled as a very lonely place to be, as there was no communal area where one could get to know other people and the atmosphere did not encourage conversation. The receptionist was the only person who knew everyone working in this setting and how everyone fitted together, so it paid "to keep on the right side of her". It was extremely difficult to contact any of the GPs who referred patients, and this particular counsellor had only one positive and truly "shared care" conversation with a GP. This counsellor said, "It took a great deal of effort to remain positive."

From the above account, it would seem that careful thought and planning would be needed to make this kind of setting both workable and pleasant as a workplace in order for the counsellor to feel part of a primary care team.

Surgery culture

This section looks at the different types of "culture" found in surgeries.

The *Concise Oxford Dictionary* defines culture as "the customs, institutions, and achievements of a particular nation, people or group". It has been my experience as a supervisor that a counsellor who works at more than one surgery can experience a very different culture in each.

Below I list the main types of surgery culture that I have either encountered personally, or have had the privilege to hear about from my supervisees.

The psychologically minded surgery culture

By this, I refer to whether there is a place within the medical ethos of the practice for an understanding of unconscious process and a willingness to take on the concepts of somatization and defence mechanisms when dealing with both patient and staff interpersonal and intrapersonal dynamics. It is often found that the lead GP sets the tone for the psychological mind-set of the practice in this area. The reader will get a feel for this at his/her initial interview. It is more likely that patients' "problems" will be medicalized in a primary care setting than in any other counselling setting. In Penny Gray's interview with psychiatrist Joanna Moncrieff, to be found in *Therapy Today* (2007a), Moncreiff cites Nikolas Rose (2003). He has written widely on this subject, and he believes that people in general society have started to medicalize their distress and have absorbed the idea of "chemical imbalance" to explain depression, anxiety, and other more florid mental illnesses, such as schizophrenia. Moncreiff says, "The problem is that the whole system is wrong. A lot of current psychiatric problems are iatrogenic, they are created not just by psychiatry but by a whole social climate that endorses a medical view of distress" (pp. 28–31).

Formal and overtly hierarchical surgery culture

By this, I refer to a culture where the lead GP is very much from the "old school", where people are addressed by their titles, that is, Mrs, Mr, etc. This includes both staff and patients, and where there is a sharp distinction in attitude between professional medical members of staff (doctors and nurses) and non-medical staff (receptionists, secretaries). In this culture, the hierarchy will be quite obvious, but this will not necessarily mean that it is not a friendly or accepting place in which to work. I believe that this set-up can be more honest, as there is no pretence that all staff carry equal responsibility and power either within or outside the practice.

The informal surgery culture

This is the opposite to the above, and can give the impression that "we are pals together". This message can be misleading, as, in practice, if it is not lived out, it can lead to hurt and resentment among the staff.

Covert hierarchical culture

This can arise as above, but new staff are not overtly informed of the culture that operates; in other words, it is the "secret" way, the subject of which is never spoken of or made explicit.

Open, friendly, welcoming, and co-operative culture

I believe this type of culture can work very well in a formal and overtly hierarchical surgery, mainly because everyone knows their position and its boundaries. However, only your personal experience over time can make this clear to you. It has been my experience that most surgery cultures are co-operative at a professional level, that is, in the best interests of the patients.

Closed, unfriendly, and non-co-operative culture

By definition, this is the opposite to the above.

The closed, unfriendly, and non-co-operative culture can occur when change within the setting is feared and unwelcome, or there have been too many changes in a short space of time.

When grown men and women come together as a group, each one brings the defence mechanisms of dependence, idealization, denial, splitting, projection, and unconscious fantasy that were learnt and laid down in their unconscious as an infant. In a group, as with individuals, change and uncertainty can raise anxiety levels. This can lead to regression and other group behaviour, for example, pairing and splitting, etc. In this regressed state, the group does not function well as an effective team.

When a counsellor is taken on in a surgery for the first time, thus destabilizing the homeostasis of the primary care team, people are often less aware of the unconscious script that is being set in motion than of the obvious benefits of having someone on site to whom GPs and others can make referrals for psychological health problems. This can leave staff puzzled and confused. What we are talking about here are transference and countertransference reaction phenomena. Some practices keep the same staff for years, or do not expand as rapidly as others in terms of taking on board visiting consultants (psychiatrists, etc.) or practitioners (physiotherapists, reflexologists, etc.) There may be a "dyed in the wool" attitude that fears and resists any kind of change.

Change is unsettling and can upset organizations in a similar way to individuals. It helps if the lead person in the practice openly acknowledges this fact, giving the message that individuals and groups of individuals will have reactions to change and that accommodation of this will take time and patience.

Diversity of personnel

As mentioned in the previous paragraphs, there can now be many different types of practitioner and consultant who visit the primary care setting. Although counsellors would not expect to know who they all are, it is possible that the visitor may refer a patient to the counsellor after consultation with the patient's GP. Each surgery will have its own referring culture in which certain designated staff can refer to the counsellor.

It is surprising how many people one may encounter in any one surgery, and this is not an exhaustive list and is not in any order of seniority or importance, but can include:

- doctors and nurses;
- psychiatrist;
- physiotherapists;
- osteopaths;
- school nurse;
- midwife;
- receptionists;
- patients;
- patients' families;
- phlebotomists;
- pharmacists;
- cleaners;
- handyman;
- deliveryman;
- counsellors.

Issues of power

Use and misuse of power within organizations and how these manifest themselves in surgeries

The power of defended anxiety and the "shadow" side of the GP, counsellor, and the whole primary care setting must always be kept in mind, as this darker side to the work can give birth to misuse of power and splitting.

The setting of the GP surgery has similarities to that of a family in the way problems arise and are solved. An individual may react to a problem or conflict in the "surgery family" that may make a situation worse rather than better. As in families, people may seek allies, try to apportion blame to others, and it is not unknown for individuals to become scapegoats, albeit at an unconscious level of intent.

A practice manager, having the responsibility of balancing the books, may find the budget for counselling competing with the budget for drugs. He/she could then go on to use this competition situation to try to reduce the counsellor's hourly rate: this could be experienced as a misuse of power, or it could just be the manager attempting to make the best of the reality that presents itself.

Tensions within generations of staff may arise, the older members perhaps resenting a new member coming in with a "new broom" and trying to sweep away some old practices that have worked for years. In these times of transition, for example, when a new member of staff is taken on or when moving to new premises, old rivalries may be resurrected. Rivalry can occur over quite small issues, for example, who will have the "best" room or parking place, etc.

The retirement of a senior partner after many decades can disrupt the homeostasis of the surgery in a similar way to a death in the family. At these times, the whole "pecking order" has to be rejigged and power may be misused.

Hawkins and Shohet (2000) define organizational culture as the different explicit and implicit assumptions and values that influence the behaviour and social artefacts of different groups. Bion (1961), when speaking of groups, proposes that some of the individual's contributions within the group come unmistakeably from him/her, but, through the medium of the group, he/she can make contributions anonymously. If the group (primary care team) provides a way for this to happen, then an individual can begin to use the group for evasion and denial. This only happens with the unconscious collusion of the group.

Example of group unconscious collusion: expression of anger and resentment

It is possible for an individual or sub-group (say, the pharmacists) to be unconsciously delegated as the avenue for the expression of anger or resentment for the rest of the team, perhaps because they are more likely to be in conflict with the "management" as a general rule. This is often seen in training organizations, where it can be the students that are seen as militant and angry.

It is easy to see how this could happen in the primary care setting. For example, when a surgery culture has evolved over many years, it is possible that certain behaviours, ideas, values, and structures are rarely challenged, as the group unconsciously sanctions them. Hence, there can be an unchallenged misuse of power. In the counsellor's experience, this could be experienced when he/she is the butt of passive aggression: for example, when a receptionist "forgets" to pass on an important message, or when a well-established sub-group, for instance, the pharmacists, are overruled by the senior partner on some important issue regarding drugs. My experience of GP surgeries leads me to consider that perhaps the answer to this may be that the unconscious processes at work need to become conscious before there can be an improvement in honest and healthy communication.

I seem to have majored upon the negative, but I will add that a wise, charismatic senior partner, who involves his/her staff at every level, can engender loyalty even through adversity, and can give a sense of mission that can capture the emotional support of the staff.

The GP's "power" transferred to the counsellor

It is easy to see that a GP may be in a very powerful position regarding patients, as he/she is invested with power by the patient. The GP may be seen as the archetypal healer, mother, or father

(Samuels, 1986). What must not be forgotten is that many patients transfer that power to the counsellor at the point of referral, or soon afterwards.

The need for the belief that someone is in control

There is another power that the surgery environment exerts, which is that of containment. It is my belief that people in general, whether in surgeries, villages, towns, or countries, have a basic need to believe that someone is in control and knows what they are doing. This originates and remains almost intact in us all from our basic dependency needs as babies and children. Few people cope with the reality that this is not always the case. Patients, when attending a surgery, are often vulnerable because of illness or emotional conflict, and, therefore, may be in a lesser or greater state of regression. This return to childlike behaviour and emotional vulnerability needs to be held and contained by the surgery. There needs to be in place a shared belief that the members of the primary care team are working together for good

Owning your professional status and identity: how do you want to be seen? How do you expect to feel?

The experienced counsellor new to the setting

This section helps the reader consider his or her own professional status. When a person enters a new environment, some regression inevitably occurs. When we consider, as counsellor, entering the new environment of the primary care setting, we must give due attention to how that regression will affect us personally and professionally. Even though we, as patients, have been visiting this particular environment for many years, it will feel both familiar and very different. It is likely that the counsellor will feel unsure and "smaller" than usual. I use the word "smaller" because I believe, as I stated earlier, that at times of change and transition, we are thrown out of our comfort zone and some infantile mechanisms can come into play. So, however experienced you are, you will be aware that you are not experienced in this setting except as a patient, with all the connotations associated with that status.

Payment for counselling

If this happens to be the first time that you have received payment for your work as a counsellor, you will be on a sharp learning curve towards owning your own professional status and beginning to feel comfortable within its "shoes". Until you value what you have to offer, it will be difficult to feel that you are a valued member of staff, even when it is obvious that other members of staff are pleased to have you on board. I have always found that to be forewarned is to be forearmed, so some work on your self-image at this level would be useful. Take some time to remind yourself what you bring to the setting and how you wish to be regarded. Knowing your boundaries and expecting them to be respected is good training for your first encounters in the setting.

Trainee placement in primary care setting

I have been privileged to supervise many clinical trainees in their placements in this setting, and feel I need to say something about their experience and emotional response. In addition to having a supervisor, it is usual for a trainee counsellor to be mentored by the lead counsellor in the surgery.

Mentoring

Much of the work in this setting is rewarding and interesting, and can give the trainee frequent job satisfaction.

Mentoring is different from supervision, and is more about supporting the trainee through the everyday running of the service. It is helpful if the lead counsellor in the primary care setting can act as a mentor to the trainee. The mentor is normally a separate person from the supervisor, and focuses more upon the context in which the counsellor works. He/she is able to provide a holding and containing function for the trainee. This often has the effect of reducing anxiety to a manageable level by mediating, on behalf of the trainee, between them and other staff and patients. The mentor should also carry out the assessments and refer patients to the trainee on grounds of competence.

It could be argued that counselling in a primary care setting is not suitable for a trainee, as they are relatively inexperienced and professionally fragile. By this, I mean that they have not yet had the experience of surviving many of the difficult counselling situations that can occur.

These challenging counselling situations are more common in the primary care setting, even when the mentor has carried out the assessment and has deemed a certain patient suitable for a trainee. However, it has been my experience that with close supervision and good mentoring, most trainees can gain important exposure to different presenting problems and personalities, and can experience a creative "survival" both for him/herself and the patient. Surviving the process of a short-term contract is very important for both counsellor and patient.

The notion of survival

Perhaps the notion of survival seems an odd one to the reader, so I will unpack it. Because the counsellor is working at "the coalface", as I have come to call counselling in the primary care setting, he/she will experience the whole spectrum of emotions, in both him/herself and the patient, that normally happen in longer-term counselling. However, in this setting, these emotions can surface much faster and in rapid succession. These strong, uncovered emotions can be alarming for both patient and counsellor in a situation where basic trust is based mainly upon the patient's trust in the primary care environment itself, rather than the person of the counsellor. Containing these emotions and the uncertainties and anxiety that they may engender can be stressful. The trainees whose surgery clinical work I have supervised were in placement for approximately six months, with a caseload of normally three patients at any one time, with a contract of five or six weeks. It has never ceased to amaze me how resilient they became. Each one of them plumbed their inner resources when challenged emotionally, which showed proof of their excellent training.

I believe that often the most challenging part for a trainee is being the new person in the primary care team. Owning one's professional status is not easy when one is inexperienced and anxious. I have found that what people find most helpful is constructive support from peers and colleagues when they share their experiences in supervision. Starting work in a new setting can sometimes feel like baptism by fire, but remember, the hotter the fire, the quicker the dross rises and can be dealt with, leaving the material (counsellor) stronger in its wake.

Knowing your way around

One way of showing your professional status is by swiftly understanding and learning how to weave your own path within the interpersonal dynamics of the primary care team. Perhaps this sounds somewhat dramatic. I guess it is a bit like learning to "win friends and influence people", and needs to be done, since you may not be welcomed with open arms by everyone. As I said earlier, it is important to discover who is the real "boss", because making a good alliance with him or her will stand you in good stead.

You also need to find out who can refer a patient to you for counselling. It can cause embarrassment if you accept a referral from a member of staff who is not in a position to make referrals. The lead GP, practice manager, or the lead counsellor, if there is one, will be able to inform you in this area. In my experience, the referrers are most likely to be GPs, nurses, and nurse practitioners.

If the practice already has a counsellor in place, there will be correct procedures for referrals. Familiarizing yourself with the correct procedures of the surgery is important for the smooth running of the service.

Record keeping

The procedure for keeping counselling records may be established before the counsellor's present employment in the surgery. If it is not, he/she needs to think carefully about how and where in the surgery building records of a patient's name, address, and attendance at counselling sessions, etc. are kept. As stated earlier, confidentiality in this setting often means confidential to the surgery, and the counsellor may wish to agree with the GPs that process notes (to be used for reflection and supervision) are kept personally, separate from the surgery building. As the courts have every right in law to subpoena a counsellor's personal notes, it may be advisable to keep only the notes needed for supervision.

Key issues

1. Each surgery or NHS Trust will have its own referring culture in which certain designated staff can refer to the counsellor.

2. The power of defended anxiety and the "shadow" side of the GP, counsellor, and the whole primary care setting must always be kept in mind, as this darker side to the work can give birth to misuse of power and splitting.

CHAPTER FIVE

Medical model *vs.* psychological model

Communication

T he medical model differs from the psychological model in many ways, not the least of these being in the area of communication, where different words can have different meanings in each model. I look at five words that may have different meanings in the two models: symptom, confidentiality, containment, boundary, and treatment. To avoid confusion, it is important that the primary care clinical staff have a grasp of the difference in these meanings.

Symptoms

In the medical model, a symptom is usually a feature that indicates a condition or disease. This may be pain, rashes, etc. Palpitations and sweaty hands could be caused by a condition of disease or by anxiety. Even when no organic origin can be found, these symptoms are often treated as though they are organic in origin and are medicated. The prescribing of medication, even when the GP suspects that the symptoms may be psychological in origin, is often the doctor's first line of treatment.

This is often done even when there is a counsellor on the primary care team, as doctors and patients alike see symptoms something to be got rid of.

As the doctor–patient relationship is often seen as an unequal one, in terms of power, the patient is used to believing that the doctor knows best and will prescribe medication.

Counsellors using either the psychodynamic or CBT approach would see symptoms more as a form of communication about the mental and/or emotional state of the patient. For some patients, the more structured and directive style of CBT fits well with their idea of doing something to "get better".

Confidentiality

The word "confidential" in the medical world means that anything spoken to a doctor or other clinical practitioner (inside or outside the primary care setting) is not shared with the general public. This can be a stumbling block for the counsellor new to the setting. He/she will be used to, and trained in, a different meaning of the word confidential. Counsellors are trained to make it clear to the client that confidential material is held more tightly than in the medical setting. A counsellor expects to share confidential information with their clinical supervisor and no other professional, unless it is felt that the person was in danger of harming themselves or others. In this instance, other professionals may need to be involved, for example, the GP, psychiatrist, and/or the mental health crisis intervention team.

This difference in interpretation of confidentiality needs to be explained to the other clinical staff in the surgery in a way that avoids them feeling threatened or undermined.

Containment

The *Concise Oxford Dictionary* defines "containment" as "the action of keeping something harmful under control". The most obvious harmful elements in the medical model are bacterial and viral infections, and cancerous tumours. In the psychological model, containment would mean providing a safe relational environment for strong emotions to be heard, understood, and processed. In the medical model, medication may be used for the containment of strong emotion and may be necessary, in addition to counselling, in order that the patient does not become harmfully overwhelmed by their feelings. One of the main functions of counselling in primary care is to provide a partnership in which as yet unknown factors can be discovered in a containing way.

Boundary

The medical and general public understanding of the word "boundary" would be a physical one, that is, within the boundary of the body, the room, or the building, etc. (slightly different in cricket!). The psychological therapy understanding of the word boundary would have to do with time and space, both internal and external to the person, in addition to the medical and everyday understanding. The notion of a person having internal boundaries, that is, boundaries within their psyche, is often an alien notion to medical staff.

A boundary can also be seen as a structure, and CBT can offer a containing structure by using and exploring the patient's cognitions in conjunction with the direction and facilitating cognitions of the counsellor.

In short-term primary care counselling, the patient, who knows consciously that he/she has a time-limited contract, will send a message to his/her unconscious (that operates timelessly) saying "you haven't got long". This will set up a conflict for the unconscious mind, as there will be both resistance and a desire to co-operate. Conflict can cause anxiety, making the counselling hour a fertile ground for growth.

There will be the same reaction to breaks in the short-term counselling as in longer-term counselling, whoever initiates those breaks, patient or counsellor. In a six-session contract, these must be addressed more openly, and immediately, as there is not the luxury of waiting for these reactions to unfold.

If a patient fails to formally cancel a session but merely does not arrive (DNAs), the ramifications of breaks in the process may be brought painfully home to him/her when the counsellor counts that break as one of the six sessions. Although the patient would be informed of these conditions of the contract in the assessment, he/she may "forget" and find these sanctions harsh. As counselling in the surgery is usually free at the point of delivery, these conditions are in place for two reasons: first, that DNAs waste the counsellor's valuable time and the surgery's resources; second, to help the patient understand and appreciate their valuable part in the process. The patient might need help to understand that consulting with a counsellor in primary care is different from consulting with their GP; the counsellor–patient relationship is a partnership, with both parties having a valuable contribution to make within the contract and in the understanding of the best way to facilitate the person moving forward in their life.

Treatment

In the medical model, the meaning of the word "treatment" is usually understood as the medical care of an illness or injury. The CBT approach to counselling fits well with this understanding, and at the assessment a treatment plan would be formulated with the patient.

Historically, the word "treatment" does not sit well with psychodynamic counsellors, even though psychodynamic theory is rooted within the psychoanalytic tradition, which uses the word "treatment" to describe the service they offer the patient. As stated above, under the heading "Boundary", the counselling relationship is seen by the counsellor (if not readily by the patient) as a partnership where the patient is not so much "done unto" as held and contained and then facilitated to find their own solutions or life pathway.

Key issues

1. Certain words differ in meaning within the medical model and the psychological therapy model.
2. Discuss the meaning of these words with the primary care staff.
3. The unconscious mind does not operate in linear time, but releases emotions felt and laid down in the past into the present. The present event or relationship triggers events and emotions from the past.

CHAPTER SIX

The primary care counsellor's support systems

Your effectiveness as a counsellor in any setting can depend considerably upon how well you feel supported. I divide this section into two: external support and internal support. External support is just as it says, relationships, structures, and systems which are in place for the counsellor, with the internal support being the counsellor's inner world and its projections. I cannot stress strongly enough the counsellor's need of personal support systems. The counsellor is a human being, and, as such, is prey to becoming emotionally vulnerable at any time.

External support

Professional support comprises collegial and peer relationships, CPD (continuing professional development), and membership of accrediting and professional bodies. In the primary care setting, staff alliances and knowledge of the unique culture of the medical organizational setting are very important. Last, but not least, your accrued body of knowledge and experience in your subject will support you.

Never forget that when working in primary care, you are subject to the same group pressures as everyone else working in that setting. You may become just as competitive, resistant, and reluctant to expose your failures, weakness, incompetence, and insecurity as the other members of staff, but you are likely to be more self-aware and have understanding of the unconscious processes at work. This self-awareness and understanding is part of your support system.

Self-awareness

Part of your self-awareness will be recognizing when you feel under pressure and knowing how you react under that pressure. Counselling in the NHS is increasingly about paperwork, proving effectiveness, fighting for your space (this may be at the everyday level of searching out a private room in which to work, or fighting to keep counselling on the agenda within the NHS).

You could be put in a position where you may have to choose from the waiting list which patient is in the most urgent need. At the same time, you may be put under pressure from one or more GPs to see their "urgent" referral first.

All this may be happening under the ever-present possibility of having your case notes subpoenaed by a Crown Court. Under this kind of pressure, knowing how to use your support networks is vital.

Reeves (1998) says,

> I believe that this need to have knowledge of the medical world, mirrors the experience of counsellors when they begin work in this setting and encounter the overwhelming impact of the medical model as offered by the other members of the primary care team. [pp. 39–40]

Reeves suggests that this can engage the counsellor in a struggle between the need to establish credibility and continuing to value the unique perspective counselling offers.

Other areas of professional support can be found in the codes of ethics or ethical frameworks of those professional bodies to which to counsellor belongs. There are clear guidelines in these works, but ones that usually leave room for the counsellor to be flexible enough so as to remain autonomous and use his/her own discretion regarding interpretation.

Casework supervision support

The counsellor will probably experience casework supervision as the major part of the external support network. It is here that the counsellor can look at his/her own thought patterns, unconscious processes, receive emotional support, and consider what of the presenting material belongs to him/her and what belongs to the patient.

Henderson (1999) says,

> As in supervision in any complex organisation, time needs to be put aside for systemic matters. Supervisors support counsellors to sustain work in the dynamic flux of roles and relationships with colleagues and clients, and to stay open to change and new ways to offer and manage a counselling service within the particular opportunities and constraints of the practice. [pp. 85–103]

The counsellor's own defences against uncovering psychic pain

Since it is generally accepted that it is the counsellor–patient relationship that is the most mutative element in the counselling process, supervision provides a safe place for both CBT and psychodynamic counsellors to be challenged by looking at the counsellor's own defences and thoughts. It is often at the assessment stage of the counselling that he/she may unconsciously defend against something the patient has disclosed. When bringing this patient to supervision, it may be discovered that the counsellor is in an unconscious collusion with the surgery's defence against uncovering psychic pain.

Crowther (2002) has observed that it is in a medical institution that other staff members may see the support of supervision as synonymous with not coping and/or that the counsellor has to be watched over carefully by his/her supervisor to make sure he/she does not make mistakes. This can lead to the counsellor (especially the trainee) feeling misunderstood or not seen as a member worthy of respect. This can be very hard to take, as the counsellor fights to keep hold of his/her feelings of professionalism, and sometimes an explanation of the use of clinical supervision may need to be given to other members of staff.

It is important for the primary care counsellor that his/her clinical supervisor embraces and values the context of the counselling under review, without being overly seduced or de-skilled by it. He/she must understand that a new and anxious counsellor, wishing to make the correct impression, may become over-anxious to get all the facts right in an assessment session so as not to miss any important pathology. Martin (2002) sees here a possible danger of the patient's voice being drowned out.

Therefore, as Curtis Jenkins (1997) believes, the supervisor should have knowledge of GP surgery counselling and preferably have worked within that setting at some time, so that he/she can understand the range of difficulties experienced and the effect on the counsellor of working as a member of a primary care team. Although I agree with Curtis Jenkins in the main, even as a supervisor who has worked in the setting, it has been my experience that my transference to the surgery in which I worked as a counsellor for five years sometimes gets in the way and can affect supervision—I have found myself projecting my past experiences with GPs on to the GPs and staff under present review brought to me by the counsellor for supervision.

The supervisor needs to help the counsellor to regularly explore his/her own contribution to the triadic relationship between counsellor, GP, and patient.

Supervision support is also useful for looking at the interpersonal dynamics of the primary care team and how they affect the counselling work.

Burton and Henderson (1997) believes that for counsellors who work in a GP surgery, issues unique to an NHS setting context must be considered and that supervision which focuses only on casework may fail to help and support the counsellor as part of a multidisciplinary team.

The "parallel process" (Mattinson, 1975)

Countertransference, when spoken about in relation to the counselling session with counsellor and client, refers to the thoughts, feelings, and behaviours of the counsellor. The parallel process refers to the unconscious process of projective identification, where unconscious fantasies, conflicts, and psychic material held unconsciously by the counsellor for the client are subsequently projected into the supervisor and are, thus, available for observation in his/her thoughts, feelings, and behaviours. Put more simply, supervisees can unconsciously present themselves to their supervisors as their client has presented to them. Searles (1986), writing in 1965, was the first to write about the parallel process, calling it the "reflection process" between therapy and supervision. Martin (2002) calls it the supervisor's "slip road" to the unconscious of both patient and supervisee.

Supervision can be used to look at the phenomenon of projective identification, that is, what the patient has unconsciously projected into the counsellor for the purpose either of communication and containment, or evacuation and evasion of psychic pain. It is in this area that there may come a blurring of boundaries between what belongs to the patient and what belongs to the counsellor. The other element of countertransference, the counsellor's transference to the patient, needs to be teased out and then taken to personal therapy for illumination there. The counsellor's countertransference is one of the most important tools for the work and an instrument of research into the patient's unconscious.

Martin (2002) says,

In psychodynamic supervision two processes occur simultaneously. One process involves the supervisor consciously supervising the actual work between supervisee and client. The other involves the supervisor engaging unconsciously with the client's material. It is this quite complex interaction which, if properly responded to, enables a furthering of unconscious communication from supervisor to supervisee, and supervisee to client, which is essentially therapeutic. [pp. 13–14]

Searles (1986) says,

The emotions experienced by a supervisor—including even his private, "subjective" fantasy experiences and his personal feelings about the supervisee—often provide valuable clarification of processes currently characterizing the relationship between the supervisee and the patient. [p. 157]

Searles sees these processes as the very ones that have been caus- ing difficulty in the therapeutic relationship. These are processes that, because they have not been recognized by the supervisee, have not been consciously and verbally brought to supervision. He says, "The processes at work currently in the relationship between patient and therapist are often reflected in the relationship between therapist and supervisor" (*ibid*.). Searles calls this the "reflection process"; Mattinson (1975) calls it the "parallel process".

Ekstein and Wallerstein's clinical rhombus (1972) and its exten- sions, as put forward by Stewart (2002), bring the specific interface between supervision and the organization (in this case, the primary care setting) into consideration (see Figure 1). For the purpose of looking at the GP surgery supervision, I change administration (A in Ekstein and Wallerstein's rhombus) for surgery (SRGY). The external supervisor's relationship with the surgery and the patient are indirect ones with two routes. The first route is via the super- visee and his/her relationship with both the patient and the surgery as a whole (which includes the individual members of that

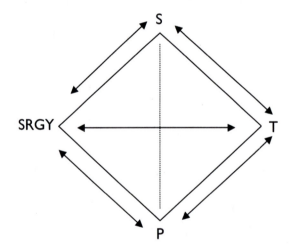

Figure 1. Adaptation of Ekstein and Wallerstein's clinical rhombus (SRGY = surgery, S = supervisor, T = therapist, P = patient).

organization, e. g., doctors, nurses, reception, etc.). The second route of relationship is through the supervisor's own transference to the surgery as a whole and his/her transferences to the individual members, originating from the supervisor's past. This route would also include the supervisor's identifications with both the supervisee and the patient, as he/she has had past experience of those two positions.

For the therapist trained only in CBT, the above will be less easy to understand, but he/she will have an appreciation of the effect of other relationships and their dynamics within the surgery setting. He/she is similarly affected by countertransference feelings, but does not use this phenomenon in the same way, although he/she will be aware that it is the relationship between therapist and patient which accounts for most that is mutative in the work.

Personal therapy

Personal therapy has, as one of its functions, an arena for considering your psychical limits. It is another forum for separating out the counsellor's material from the patient material. If and when it has been identified in supervision that the counsellor has transference issues with the patient and has had the opportunity to make a distinction between what material belongs to the patient and what material belongs to the counsellor, he/she is well advised to take the "problem" to personal therapy. If the counsellor is not currently in therapy, it is useful to discuss the issue with an experienced and trusted colleague. None of us is without unanalysed areas of our inner world, and we must always accept that we are vulnerable in this area. Long experience in the field does not immunise you from contamination or inner conflict.

The counsellor's personal support network

A support network comprises all that is supportive in the counsellor's private life, for example, family bonds, friendships, insight and self-awareness, hobbies and interests, and knowing your limits, both psychical and physical. A counsellor's own therapy has, as one of its functions, an arena for considering psychical limits. It is important that the counsellor does not gain all his/her emotional gratification from patients. A healthy and stable personal network is invaluable for assisting the counsellor to separate from his/her work.

Internal support

Internal support comprises support that is derived from the counsellor's inner world; the world of inner objects and inner boundaries guided by unconscious processes, the strengthening and knowledge of which can enhance a counsellor's ego strength in the face of emotionally charged situations in the primary care setting.

A counsellor's inner objects are the internalized relationships, both good and bad, that have been set down in infancy. These will have been mitigated and constellated anew through everyday life and personal therapy into a more mature and healthy "family" in his/her inner world.

Inner boundaries are those psychic structures that enable us to remain separate from the projections of others. These inner psychic boundaries may be breached by our patients' unconscious projections, but our strength lies in how successfully we can recognize those breaches and reset the boundaries.

It is through a thorough personal therapy and regular supervision that the counsellor's internal support system can be kept strong and healthy.

Waiting lists and their supportive function

Waiting lists can be organized in ways that can be either helpful or unhelpful. Obviously, it is best to have them organized in a helpful way that feels supportive to counsellors, patients, and other members of staff. It is important that this "problem" is addressed within the primary care team so that it can be a joint responsibility. For a counsellor to hold a three to six-month waiting list can be stressful.

With close collaboration and transparency between counselling and referring staff, waiting lists can be managed in a client-centred way. By this, I mean offering counselling on a "needs basis" rather than a strict adherence to "first come, first served". A patient's need for counselling can be measured during the assessment process. This is necessary, as referring members of staff can feel that a patient has urgent needs when actually they are able to wait.

Ways to make the waiting list manageable

- If you are the only counsellor in the primary care team, enlist another interested party, for example, your mentor, if you have one, the lead GP, or practice manager, to talk over issues such as urgency of referral, appropriate ways to contact patients, management of holiday cover, patients who DNA frequently, and when to write to patients regarding waiting times. You will find there are issues that come up that are particular to your surgery or health centre. The mentor is a separate person from the supervisor and focuses more upon the context in which the counsellor works.
- Have some control over the number of referrals by knowing who can refer patients to you for counselling and a way of informing them that you may close the waiting list when it reaches a certain size.
- Remember that rigid waiting lists help no one. Stacey (2003) proposes,

> It has been recognised for a long time that bureaucratic control is neither rational nor efficient outside certain limited conditions and that it produces a number of negative behavioural consequences that undermine its effectiveness. [p. 69]

- Burton and Henderson (1997) suggests we are aware that some patients will need an extension of number of sessions and this will put pressure on the waiting list. This must be taken into consideration when offering a patient more sessions.
- Have a standard letter ready to send out when a patient has been on the waiting list for some time and a way for them to inform you if they no longer need to be seen.

- Bear in mind that a GP's sense of urgency and immediacy is not always an indication of the patient's need, and with suitable consultation between counsellor and GP, the "emergency" may be contained by a holding letter. I deal with the issues of urgency, holding, and containment in the next chapter.
- Discussion of waiting lists in supervision can alleviate pressure and also identify when the "burden" of the list is affecting the counselling work currently being done.

Ethical issues

Guggenbuhl-Craig (1996) suggests that it is likely that patients will put considerable pressure on the GP to betray the Hippocratic Oath (to benefit and not hurt or wrong a patient). What this means is that when under this pressure, the GP may unconsciously collude with the patient by not pointing out the largely psychic origin and emotional components of his/her presenting ailment. Guggenbuhl-Craig considers that the average doctor, by this omission, encourages his patients to emphasize even more the somatic aspects of their emotional problems. He says, "If the symptoms improve, he is the great healer; if they deteriorate, it is obvious that the patient has failed to carry out his instructions" (Guggenbuhl-Craig, 1996, p. 22). Guggenbuhl-Craig puts forward that a therapist's tools are his honesty, genuineness, and his personal contact with the unconscious, but that there is a shadow side to this; the therapist is prey to the same transference to the doctor, his power, opinions, and other processes put into action through the experience of working in a GP surgery. Also, due to the patient's perception of the therapist's knowledge of the human psyche, he/she can be seen as omniscient and even, at one level, the therapist can come to believe that of him/herself. Therapists have the power to be unconsciously destructive, and often there is little warning from the patient that this is happening. This is what Guggenbuhl-Craig calls the professional shadow. Regular consultation with a supervisor is the best way to deal with this problem ethically.

The BACP Ethical Framework and the Codes of Ethics and Practice of other professional bodies provide guidelines for the protection of patients (and, I believe, counsellors), but leave some room for interpretation and individuality for counsellors subscribing to them.

Key issues

1. Your effectiveness as a counsellor in any setting can depend considerably upon how well you feel supported. Thorough personal therapy and regular supervision keep the counsellor's internal support system (psychic boundaries) strong and healthy.
2. The counsellor is a human being and, as such, is prey to becoming emotionally vulnerable at any time.
3. Never forget that when working in the primary care setting, you are subject to the same group pressures as everyone else.
4. Supervision support is useful for looking at the interpersonal dynamics of the primary care team and how they affect the counselling work.
5. Personal therapy has, as one of its functions, an arena for considering your psychical limits. It is another forum for separating the counsellor's material from the patient material.
6. A healthy and stable personal support network is invaluable for assisting the counsellor to separate from his/her work.
7. Waiting lists can be part of a supportive system.

CHAPTER SEVEN

Whose needs are being met?

T his chapter is about recognizing whose needs are being met by a referral to counselling. This assessment of need may begin before the clinical assessment of the patient.

The GP's needs

As I have mentioned earlier, a patient's symptoms, emotions, or behaviour can arouse distress and/or unease in a GP, other referring member of staff, or a patient's family members. Sometimes, it is difficult to divine whose distress is actually being displayed. By this, I do not mean that the patient is not distressed, but he/she may be containing and/or acting out a family or marital problem; in other words, they become the person identified as the patient. Sometimes, this is obvious to the GP treating the patient, and some useful work can be done, in consultation with the counsellor, to try to identify the best course of action and/or therapy for the whole family or couple, in addition to helping the "identified patient". The identified patient may be unconsciously containing and displaying strong emotions and conflicts for other members of his/her family. I use the word "contain" here referring to the term and meaning contributed by Bion (1962a,b, 1970), that of "container–contained". I elaborate on this concept later in the text.

When the patient's problem, symptoms, or distress echo or resonate with something in the GP's own past or present distress, thus making the referral feel urgent to the GP, the counsellor needs to approach the situation with extra tact and sensitivity. If the counsellor is new to the practice, it may be prudent to accept the referral as "urgent", since he/she will not be in the privileged position of having gained experience in understanding the different referring styles of the GPs in the practice.

The "difficult" patient

Most GPs have at least one patient in his/her caseload that they find particularly difficult. In this instance, the GP's heart sinks when the person enters his/her consulting room. The counsellor is more likely to have this type of patient referred for counselling during the first year of a new counselling service in the primary care setting. This is often because the GP can, at last, "off-load" the patient on to the counsellor for containment. The types of problem that this category of patient displays are often social in origin rather than medical. Their distress is genuine, but their problems are often intractable.

Example: Dr Peter and Derek

Dr Peter is very efficient in his work and tries very hard to keep to time with his appointments. Derek is an unemployed, middle-aged man living with his elderly parents. Derek is his parents' carer and, as they become older, they need a lot of attention. He comes frequently to see Dr Peter with both minor ailments, which could be self-medicated, and depression due to his unfulfilled life. He has been consulting with Dr Peter since he was a boy. Dr Peter would like to be able to help Derek and has given him advice about what might be available through Social Services to make his life easier with his parents. Derek tells Dr Peter that the reason he has no job and is not married is because he has to look after his parents.

Dr Peter has seen the flaw in Derek's thinking, but cannot bring himself to suggest that it might be the other way around: that is, Derek is frightened of commitment to a job or marriage. When a counsellor is taken on in the surgery, Dr Peter refers Derek for counselling. It is unlikely that a six-week contract would be long enough to tackle Derek's deep-seated problem.

Intractable social problems

When a patient like Derek brings what seem to be intractable social problems, the counsellor or GP must assess whether it is the personality of the patient that adds to perpetuating and exacerbating the problem, or whether, with suitable support and help towards a greater self-awareness and insight into the dynamics of the situation, the patient can become less distressed and feel more in control of his/her life.

Also, with certain personality traits or high dependency needs, some patients may need to receive counselling in the form of a short-term contract whenever they are overwhelmed by times of change or transition. This arrangement can hold some patients who may otherwise be hospitalized or be in need of involvement by Social Services. I use the word "hold", here, using the meaning as developed by Winnicott (1956). I elaborate on this concept later in the text.

The patient's family's need

I look briefly here at the phenomenon of the "identified patient", using psychodynamic, CBT, and systems theory.

Psychodynamic approach

As I have mentioned earlier, Bion (1961) puts forward, when speaking about groups, that some individuals can make contributions anonymously, using the other group members to express their emotions by use of unconscious processes. If we think of the family or couple as a "group" this same unconscious collusion can occur.

The family can unconsciously decide to "use" one family member to express distress and conflict for the rest of the family. The same can occur with couples, where one spouse, because of his/her ability to contain strong emotion projected from the other, is unconsciously selected to contain what is projected. This process, in psychodynamic terms, is named projective identification. If the spouse containing the strong emotion for the other (for instance, anger, fear, or depression) acts this out in an unacceptable way, it is likely that they will become the identified patient and be referred for counselling. Having said that, these kinds of unconscious processes are going on all the time in all relationships, and as long as each performs the function in turn and appropriately, life can be relatively harmonious.

A CBT approach

As the patient tells their story in the assessment session, it may become clear that the patient and his family share beliefs that are irrational: they do not stand up to reasoning, or beliefs that lead to automatic negative thoughts, such as "the world ought to be fair, there ought to be justice, our family are always the under-dogs". In a situation like this, the "identified patient" may be the family member who is either most distressed or most determined to change. When working with this person, the reader must remember that neither the patient nor the counsellor will find it easy to challenge these beliefs without considerable support.

A systems theory approach

This approach, which is based upon communication theory, may be useful in the primary care setting when looking at the notion of the "identified patient". This is an approach that sees the family as a system in which the members unconsciously collude with a particular script or myth about themselves as a family. Each individual who is part of the family system has a different story to tell about the "problem". They each have different beliefs attached to the "problem" and can see his/her part in it from a unique angle. This approach looks at problems within the system of relationships in which they occur, and aims to promote change by intervening in the broader system rather than in the individual alone (Burnham, 1998). This approach has been used by psychiatry, social work, and nursing, to a lesser or greater degree. A GP who has known the family and the individuals who comprise it for a number of years may be able to see what the family are doing to themselves: that is, what the family are achieving at an unconscious level. He/she may have seen, over time, the difference between stories told and stories lived. The GP may see the collusion at work before his/her eyes over the years, or may feel happy to look at this possibility with the counsellor in order to help the family towards a healthier way of being together, especially the person suffering and displaying distress behaviour. Analysing problems, as presented by the "identified patient", in terms of interactional patterns means that change needs to happen in the areas of patterns, behaviours, and beliefs.

Example: John and his headaches

John had been a patient in the practice for about fifteen years, and, over this time, had complained of being depressed, tense, and having headaches. He had received antidepressants and seen a psychiatrist. The headaches persisted, and the GP referred him to the primary care counsellor. The counsellor quickly decided this was a family problem, and helped John to produce a genogram (a drawing completed between the counsellor and patient to indicate, in symbol form, the patient's past and present relationships and relationships between other family members). The counsellor explained how this might help their understanding of their problem. The counsellor picked up that John became stressed and defensive when they talked of his family of origin. His father had died when he was very small, and he described his mother as being depressed and moody. While he was still a small boy, his mother remarried into an already dysfunctional family—"they were all mad" was how John described them.

The counsellor soon became aware that John knew nothing of his father's family, and encouraged him to make some enquiries. He soon discovered that he had an aunt, uncle, and cousins, his father's sister and family, living in the next village. He contacted them, and was welcomed and told of what a happy and sane man his father had been. Subsequently, he was able to reframe himself as at least partly normal, and his headaches began to become less frequent.

The counsellor's need

One would hope that an experienced counsellor working within a primary care team would have discovered his/her areas of vulnerability regarding their own needs, be those of dependency, belonging, status, or fiscal needs, and would handle them appropriately. However, it is important the counsellor is ever vigilant with regard to his/her own supervision and/or personal therapy in order to uncover any unhelpful collusion or over-identification. The trainee counsellor is particularly susceptible to unconsciously meeting his/her needs in their first counselling setting. It is here that I will talk about Bion's idea of the "container–contained".

This, I believe, is a good point at which to introduce the well-documented notion that the counsellor or therapist contains projected unconscious thoughts and fantasies from the patient's psyche in his/her own psyche during the contract of counselling via the mechanism of projective identification. He/she is then in a good position to modify them to a more bearable system. The patient can then introject these more bearable elements, over time. I will speak more about how this works for the patient under the next section but I cannot stress strongly enough how important it is for the counsellor, trainee or experienced, to work at separating counsellor need from patient need through vigilance and supervision. We aim to work therapeutically. Sometimes, as counsellors, we gain greatly from and with our patients, but we must never knowingly gain from a patient's need except in the way that we are fiscally rewarded through our employment, and professionally by extending our experience. This ethical aim is as important as the Hippocratic Oath is for doctors.

The patient's need

A patient in any counselling setting has the need and the right to be held and contained. Earlier, I briefly mentioned Bion's notion of the "container–contained". Here, I elaborate upon what that can mean for the patient. I also look at the notion of "holding" as put forward by Winnicott. Ogden (2004) sees the "container–contained" addressing not what we think, but the way we think; that is, how we process lived experience and what occurs psychically when we are unable to do psychological work with that experience. Ogden believes that fundamental to Bion's thinking on the container–contained is the idea of "the psycho-analytic function of the person-ality" (Bion, 1962a, p. 89). Ogden thinks that, in introducing this term, Bion is suggesting "that the human personality is constitu-tionally equipped with the potential for a set of mental operations that serves the function of doing conscious and unconscious psychological work on emotional experience (a process that issues in psychic growth)" (Ogden, 2004, p. 1355).

How this works out for the patient in primary care

So, we must think how this works out for the patient in primary care receiving short-term counselling. It is my belief that, in this setting, the counsellor is part of the whole primary care en-vironment as well as part of the primary care team. By this, I mean the environment that a patient enters, both externally and internally, is as much an internalization of the GP settings over many years as it is the actual building he/she enters. Since Bion's notion of the "container–contained" is generally applied to long-term therapy, we must see how this "containment" is achieved in the primary care setting. Think, for a moment, about how you feel visiting your GP when you are feeling ill or distressed. Unless you have had a very traumatic experience involving your GP, you will probably feel that the GP surgery is somewhere that you will be helped to feel better, either physically or emotionally. Why will you think that? Probably because you have internalized the primary care environment, over the years, as a safe and gen-erally helpful place, a holding and containing place. You may feel upset when the advice or procedures the GP is able to suggest for you do not work, but you still go back because it is your first port of call and the place where you expect to be heard and healed.

Here, I have introduced the notion of "holding". This is a concept of the psychoanalyst Winnicott (1956). Ogden (2004) says, "the word 'holding', as used by Winnicott, is strongly evocative of images of the mother tenderly and firmly cradling her infant in her arms, and, when he is in distress, tightly holding him against her chest" (p. 1350). Ogden suggests that the concept of "holding", for Winnicott, is an ontological concept that he uses to explore specific qualities of the experience of being alive at different development stages, as well as the changing intrapsychic–interpersonal means by which the sense of continuity of being is sustained over time. I think the operative word here is "continuity". What the primary care environment offers to patients is continuity of place and time, that is, it can be located geographically and is there when we need it, just as a mother is there when we are infants. It makes us feel safer.

So, although we cannot usually offer long-term counselling in the GP surgery, the primary care environment can provide long-term holding and containment

Key issues

1. Patients with certain personality traits or high dependency needs may need to receive counselling in the form of a short-term contract whenever they are overwhelmed by times of change or transition
2. We aim to work therapeutically. Sometimes, we, as counsellors, gain greatly from and with our patients, but we must never knowingly gain from a patient's need except in the way we are fiscally rewarded through our employment. This ethical aim is as important as the Hippocratic Oath is for doctors
3. A patient in any counselling setting has the need and the right to be held and contained.

PART II

THE PRACTICE OF COUNSELLING AND THE IMPACT OF THE SETTING

THEORY AND PRACTICE: WORKING AT THE "COALFACE"

Introduction to Part II

Throughout the following chapters, medical and psychiatric terms are used. This may be anathema to some counsellors, but the reality is that in a medical setting these terms will be used and need to be understood, in order that members of the primary care team have a shared understanding of their meaning and possible symptoms related to them.

This section aims to facilitate the counsellor's ability to be knowledgeably flexible in the use of short-term models adapted for use in a primary care setting, based upon psychodynamic and CBT thinking. Counselling contracts based upon psychodynamic and CBT thinking are suitable in the primary care setting because not all patients referred for counselling fit neatly into a counsellor's preferred model of working. We should not be surprised at this, as patients are unique in their psychic makeup and life situations. Social situations are myriad, and each person is at a different place in their lifespan, emotional development, and life journey.

As the counsellor becomes more experienced within the setting, he/she will become more creative in what he/she has to offer patients. The reader will develop his/her own style in dealing with the interpersonal dynamics of the setting and begin to know how and when risks can be taken without damage to themselves or their patients. By this, I mean the reader will begin to trust his/her intuition about certain situations and presenting problems. The trainee on placement would do well to rely heavily on the wisdom of their mentor and their supervisor, while beginning to forge a style that is comfortable and authentic for them. The trainee may discover some of their hidden talents and gain valuable experience in the primary care setting.

Patients in the primary care setting are not usually "expert clients", that is, they have not received counselling before, and an explanation of what counselling is and how it works may be necessary. Often, we need to explain that counselling is not giving advice. This may seem to be stating the obvious, but it is surprising how many counsellors, when setting the contract, take it for granted that the patient will know what counselling is and how it works.

The counsellor in any setting needs to be able to distinguish between sadness, unhappiness, and depression. As Freud told us, there is ordinary human misery, which for some is a normal, healthy response to terrible situations. It is important that we do not make a patient's normal reaction into pathology.

Where we aim to make a difference is by attempting to begin a process within the individual where, as Symington writes in his book, *Emotion and Spirit*, "constructive action replaces destructive action". By this, Symington means attending to the mental pain and suffering that issues from something the person is "doing". Often, the person does not know what they are "doing", and needs help to discover it and to begin to change (Symington, 1994, p. 192). The word "doing", in this instance, means as much a way of being and relating to others as carrying out an action. I think what Symington is talking about here is the neurotic re-enactment that we so often see in the consulting room. The term "neurotic re-enactment" is a psychoanalytical reference to the repetition of some behaviour, thought process, or feeling that was set up in the past, but is maladaptive and unhelpful to the person in the present.

The CBT counsellor will be familiar with how the patient's conscious thoughts, feelings, and behaviour, stemming from core beliefs set up in childhood, manifest themselves in a person's life and in the counselling sessions. Symington speaks of moving towards an inner autonomy within the counsellor and the patient, from which freedom can flow.

CHAPTER EIGHT

Time and how we use it: assessing what is appropriate for the patient

By whichever model of counselling the reader is guided, this seems a good place to talk about the importance of time. Most counsellors agree that the concept of time is important and that we, as humans, are not just as we seem in the moment, but that our lives are influenced by our past experiences as well as our ideas about our present and future. Whatever we wish to call this phenomenon, our behaviours are not only ruled by our conscious thoughts and feelings. We, as therapists, have a duty of care to embrace this concept fully for our patients. As Mann says, "One way of understanding the failure to give time central significance in short forms of psychotherapy lies in the will to deny the horror of time by the therapists themselves" (Mann, 1973, p. 10).

Mann believes that any time-limited therapy must recognize that child time and adult time are in the counselling arena, that is, children experience time differently from adults. This fact can give rise to powerful conflicting reactions, responses, and expectations, as the inner child of the person wants and expects as much time as he/she needs, whereas time in the adult world is often rationed and limited. For example, if we are making a meal that requires several ingredients and we discover that one crucial ingredient is nowhere to be found, we may swear or kick the cat. Most people would agree that this behaviour falls within the bounds of normal. But, for some people in certain situations, their reactions may be excessive and harmful either to themselves or someone else.

Regarding the contract between patient and counsellor, Mann argues that the greater the ambiguity as to the duration of the contract, the greater the influence of child time on unconscious wishes and expectations. He has seen that the greater the specificity of duration of the therapy, the more rapidly and appropriately is child time confronted with reality and the work to be done. In other words, do not give a patient the impression they have all the time in the world when in reality they have limited time. It should be added that some people cannot or will not hear that they have limited time with the counsellor, and this has to be worked with as creatively as possible.

Types of time-limited contract found to be useful in the primary care setting

Psychodynamic brief focused counselling

The three major ingredients that make psychodynamic counselling brief are: early confrontation of the resistance, high activity on the part of the counsellor, and the counsellor's overall attitude to conducting brief counselling: keeping the end point central to the work (Molnos, 1995).

This approach can be used when a satisfactory psychodynamic formulation can be made and the client is ready to receive and make use of time-limited counselling. This works well when there is a clear focus and the client has insight and self-awareness. The work may be focused around the central conflict that is producing the present distress. This central conflict may become obvious to the counsellor during the process of making a psychodynamic formulation, or, if a psychodynamic formulation cannot be made in the assessment, the counsellor will hold the idea of a possible central conflict in mind, while looking with the patient at the conscious reason for seeking help. I cover making a psychodynamic formulation in the next chapter.

Mann lists four basic universal conflict situations:

- independence versus dependence;
- activity versus passivity;
- adequate self-esteem versus diminished or loss of self-esteem;
- unresolved or delayed grief. [Mann, 1973, p. 25]

The above central or core conflicts are common to us all. They represent and stem from the normal human developmental milestones that we have all had to negotiate, some more successfully than others: they are the emotional positions to which we may return psychically at times of regression due to illness, change, loss, and transition.

Examples of how the above four central conflicts may manifest

Independence vs. dependence

Perhaps the simplest example of regression with which we can all identify is at times of illness or a hospital admission. Perhaps we are happy to be dependent upon others at these times, and it is as we recover from illness that we have to re-find where our comfortable balance or equilibrium stands on the dependence–independence spectrum. Seen from a more emotional perspective, "dependence *vs.* independence" is about how much we are prepared to take responsibility for our own actions and emotional responses. In other words, how much are we prepared to be responsible for ourselves and how much do we expect others to take for us? We have all heard a sentence beginning with "he made me feel angry", or "she made me feel guilty". Taking responsibility for ourselves includes how we feel and how we behave.

Activity vs. passivity

This can be closely linked with the above, but not always. It is often at times of stress and change that a person may revisit a past and normally hidden inner conflict. A person may feel trapped in a situation where they feel "damned" if they take a certain action and "damned" if they take no action. In other words, always wrong. The word "action", here, is used to mean not just physical action, but also emotional response. This trap, they feel, renders them unable to help either themselves or others. Anger is often the underlying emotion, which may be played out actively or passively. This familiar strong emotion of anger may be directed outward as blame at the world in general for not meeting and fulfilling unmet needs, or directed inward, resulting in depression.

Adequate self-esteem vs. diminished, or loss of, self-esteem

When a person feels they are not coping adequately with their life, one of the overwhelming emotions may be shame. Shame is an early and deep-rooted emotion. It may be argued that the feeling of shame is inherent in being a child. Loving and encouraging parents can mitigate this sense of shame at being small and of not being able to do things well. People who have carried unmitigated shame since childhood will often apologize for coming for counselling and feel they are not worthy of help. Some feel they need to apologize for being alive at all.

Apart from shame, the root of this conflict may be how comfortable or uncomfortable a person feels with their own sense of power. People may feel threatened by their perception of their own and other people's power. Although this perception is often laid down early in life and perpetuated in subsequent relationships, it can be challenged. In the assessment, the counsellor must attempt to gauge the person's ability to be challenged within the counselling and also how strongly that may happen. This will depend upon the patient's ego strength and support network. This is looked at in more depth in the next chapter.

Unresolved or delayed grief

This conflict or situation can lie very deeply hidden and requires counsellor and patient to listen carefully to clues given in the narrative. The sense of relief and moving on that can occur when a patient is able to uncover this unresolved or delayed grief can amaze both patient and counsellor. A young mother who had suffered a cot death with her first child and then gone on to have two normal, healthy children, presented with marital problems and depression. Once she had been heard and had grieved for her son, who had died ten years previously, she came alive in a way that had seemed impossible to both her and her family.

Short-term CBT counselling

A short-term CBT counselling contract can be used with well-motivated patients who can think in an organized way. As with the short-term psychodynamic approach, the counsellor must make a judgement on how and when they may challenge the patient. They must also pay careful attention to how the patient can use language. It is a person's core beliefs about themselves, about others, and about the world that may need to be confronted. Core beliefs are deeply held and may not be apparent at a conscious level of thinking. They are more likely to be apparent in a person's negative automatic thoughts (NATs) or the "rules" that they live by. In both CBT and psychodynamic approaches, meaning plays a central role. The patient does not need to be highly articulate or intellectual to make use of CBT. However, the counsellor and patient must enter into a partnership to investigate and uncover what different concepts and words mean for the patient. CBT may include structured sessions and "homework" to be carried out between sessions. This "homework" may include rehearsing thoughts and behaviours in different ways to those that are habitual for this person. As the name CBT suggests, this approach involves attempting to change cognitions as a way of facilitating a change in feelings and behaviour. Some time is spent at the assessment uncovering a person's core beliefs, NATs, and maintenance cycles (vicious circles of thought and behaviour). For instance, a person may discover that they have a core belief that they are not worth listening to. In the assessment session, it may come to light that in their relationships they rarely or never initiate either a conversation or an activity. Their "homework" for the week may simply be to try out what it feels like to initiate one conversation or one activity with a person of their choice.

Other examples of core beliefs are "I am bad", "people are dangerous and unpredictable", "the world is full of bad things", and "life's cruel and unfair" (Willson & Branch, 2006).

I cover conceptualization of a case and making a treatment plan in the next chapter.

People often consult the counsellor saying they are not coping. This phrase needs unpacking, as people frequently feel they cannot cope any more with either a situation or physical symptom. The counsellor may help to facilitate a state of mind where, instead of the person looking at what is not coped with, they can begin to look at what they have coped with. It is often the fact that someone else is taking them and their problems seriously that initiates the shift in thinking (and coping).

It may be useful to look with the patient at Karpman's "drama triangle" (Karpman, 1968). This triangle has at its points the roles of persecutor, rescuer, and victim. This simple illustration can sometimes help a person to move out of their habitual role, thus changing the dynamics of their intimate or work relationships. The patient will need encouragement to practise this task, and may only be able to achieve a shift in one area of his/her life, for example, at work or at home.

A word of caution is that the counsellor needs to be mindful that they do not unconsciously take up one of the roles with the patient.

Brief solution-focused counselling

This can be used in conjunction with either of the above types of contract when the person is well motivated to change, is not in crisis, and can think coherently. This type of counselling can make use of the psychodynamic formulation or case conceptualization in an assessment to establish with the patient how they have found solutions to difficult situations and problems in the past, and how helpful/unhelpful those solutions have been. For instance, through gentle questioning, the counsellor and patient may discover that the person's habitual way of solving a problem may be to always try to please others. The counsellor might suggest some joint investigation into how this approach to others does not always have the desired outcome, or may even be impossible to achieve. It will usually be when the patient's habitual approach causes insoluble problems for him/her that he/she may present for counselling.

Another approach may be to help the patient identify a time when they solved a problem in a way that felt satisfactory for them, and then try to apply the steps of that solution to the current problem.

Crisis counselling

When a patient presents as regressed and in a high state of anxiety about themselves or their life, it is likely that they are in crisis. This may concern an event that is happening in the person's life involving their relationships, for example, desertion by spouse, or a trauma such as diagnosis of a terminal illness, or after a road traffic accident. The assessment may often be difficult, and perhaps needs to spread over two sessions in order to give the person time to tell their crisis story. It is important to establish what the person has in place for support outside of the surgery and between the sessions, and whether they have suicidal thoughts. Since the person may be thinking in an irrational way, it may be best practice to have a focus for each session, rather than an overall focus, in addition to helping them enlist further support where appropriate and necessary. For example, one focus may be finding somewhere to sleep that night, or enabling them to telephone a friend or relative who can support them during the next few hours or days. In certain instances, it may be necessary to seek out a GP to attend them before they leave the surgery, as they may need medication or hospitalization.

Supportive counselling

Counselling can help support someone through a short difficult phase in his/her life: for example, if someone has a court hearing pending or is going through a difficult time of change, transition, or loss. Supportive counselling may also be needed on a cyclical basis, such as a six-week contract every year. This is useful for a patient who becomes distressed or enters a state of high anxiety and crisis whenever he/she encounters change or transition in their life. This may need to happen for many years, and, in some cases, this may need to happen for the rest of their lives. These people are often disabled emotionally by early trauma and/or abuse or suffer from a personality disorder. This counselling may involve recognizing, reinforcing, and helping to strengthen the person's coping mechanisms. It has been my experience that GPs are often supportive of this arrangement. This scenario is a good example of how the holding environment of the whole primary care team can work really effectively.

Single session counselling

Single session counselling using a CBT or psychodynamic approach can be very useful in helping someone gain some clarity of thought or feeling on one specific issue. For example, choosing between different medical procedures, job offers, study options, or a decision about termination of a pregnancy. A follow-up session can be arranged if necessary. A single session can also be useful in pointing someone in the right direction for longer-term counselling if they have already decided that this is what they want.

Assessment and preparation for a referral to longer-term counselling

Assessment and preparation for longer-term counselling will often take longer than one session. Even when it becomes quite obvious to both the counsellor and patient that the way forward is to seek longer-term psychodynamic counselling or cognitive behavioural therapy, the person may need some ongoing support in finding the right counsellor and making the transition to longer-term work. For example, acute distress over a particular event may bring someone to see the primary care counsellor, but once the immediate distress is contained it may become clear that the person has deeper issues that make coping with everyday life very difficult. It is these issues that may take longer to understand and integrate.

Assessment for a psychiatric referral

Occasionally, a GP may feel unsure of a patient's state of mind, as a ten-minute consultation is often not enough time to make this type of judgement. If he/she feels that the counsellor is sufficiently knowledgeable and experienced, he may ask for his/her opinion on the matter. This kind of assessment may involve between one and six sessions. Over a period of weeks, psychotic or disorganized thinking may be uncovered, whereas in one session it may not. Most primary care settings are not able to offer therapy for someone who is psychotic, or has a disorganized personality or attachment issues. The person may have "pockets" of psychotic thinking: for instance, believing that all people in uniform are out to get them, but that other people are quite benign. This thinking only becomes apparent as the person begins to tell their story.

Someone who has had severe problems in forming attachments may appear to have some psychotic thinking as they become increasingly anxious about life and relationships, but they are less easily helped with medication. This is because poor ability to form attachments to others is seen as a personality issue rather than a mental health issue. However, medication may be prescribed to help contain anxiety.

Psychosis

Laplanche and Pontalis (1988) suggest that, in clinical psychiatry, the concept of psychosis may cover a whole range of mental illness, but that the common denominator of the psychoses lies in a primary disturbance of the libidinal relation to reality. They suggest that the majority of the manifest symptoms, and particularly delusional constructions, are secondary attempts to restore the link with objects.

Doctors working in primary care will normally recognise florid symptoms of psychosis in surgery consultation. These usually manifest themselves as hallucinations, as seen in schizophrenia, grandiosity and/or despair, as seen in bipolar disorders, and paranoia, as seen in paranoid disorders. They are usually able to make a referral to a psychiatrist for assessment or, if necessary, get the person admitted to an appropriate safe place, for example, a psychiatric hospital. However, on occasions, a GP may have a suspicion that a person has some psychotic thinking or beliefs, and he/she may feel that a six-week assessment with a counsellor may uncover this, as more time can spent with the patient in a relaxed setting. It would not be advisable to ask a counsellor on their training placement to carry out this type of assessment, as they are unlikely to have enough experience of a wide range of presentations.

A patient who has suffered from untreated depression for many years, or has been recently traumatized, for whatever reason, and is suffering severe anxiety, can display confused and muddled thinking, which may be mistaken for psychosis. Help in the form of short- or longer-term medication can be useful to bring the person to a point where they can make use of counselling.

Recognizing psychotic thinking

It is relatively easy for a patient who is not floridly psychotic to "fool" his/her GP, albeit unconsciously. Thoughts and behaviours that seem to most people to be out of touch with reality are the patient's responses to the reality they are experiencing. This thinking may be confined to certain areas of a person's life and, thus, not obviously observed in everyday conversations or situations. The thinking may be paranoid in nature, and the person's ideas about a certain event or relationship is always fixed, adamant, inflexible, and not open to attempts at reasoning by the counsellor.

Freud wrote,

> The problem of psychosis would be simple and perspicuous if the ego's detachment from reality could be carried through completely. But this seems to happen only rarely, or perhaps never. Even in a state so far removed from the reality of the external world as one of hallucinatory confusion, one learns from patients after their recovery that at the time in some corner of their mind (as they put it) there was a sane person hidden, who, like the detached spectator, watched the hubbub of illness go past him. [Freud, 1940a, p. 201]

An example of psychotic thinking manifesting in the counselling room

A person may be articulate and talking quite lucidly about their life and can even appear to be quite insightful, when into the conversation they slip something like, "So, because the two street-lights always line up when I get to a certain part of the street, I know the aliens are not far away." When asked "What aliens?", they may look quizzical and answer, "You know, the ones that always hide outside the surgery when I visit the doctor—you must have seen them." If challenged on this and asked, "How do you know they are aliens?" they may reply, as if you are quite mad, "Because they just are, everyone knows that!"

Contra-indications for short-term counselling

At the present time, the usual preferred length of a primary care contract is assessment session plus six ongoing fifty-minute sessions. Burton (1998) has identified some potential negative outcomes of this model.

- Borderline patients who become attached to their therapist at the first or second session may make a serious suicide attempt when discharged after six weeks because they perceive the termination as abandonment. Often, in these cases, six sessions will not have helped and may be damaging to the patient.
- Other patients who do not feel helped by six sessions may then be passed from one clinician to another, each of whom is not able to offer the kind of help to address underlying issues. This is often because no one has undertaken an in depth assessment. Burton believes that this may be because there is an underlying personality disorder and/or additional pathology.
- At the end of six sessions, the patient may feel a little better but says that counselling has not changed anything. As they are rarely prepared to go forward with longer-term counselling, these patients often relapse or develop new symptoms.
- When a counsellor has not undergone a rigorous training and therapy of their own. In my experience, it is unwise to try to work with a six-session model unless you have had a recognized training and clinical experience of counselling long-term with patients. The counsellor needs to be able to recognise deep-seated problems and when to recommend specialist help, for example, with eating disorders (Burton, 1998).

Key issues

1,   The concept of time is important. We are not just as we seem in the moment, our lives are influenced by our past and our ideas about present and future.

2.   In short-term counselling, it is important to recognize and assess "core beliefs" (CBT) and "central conflicts" (psychodynamic).

3.   When a person is in crisis they will be regressed and anxious.

4.   Patients who have suffered early trauma may need times of supportive counselling throughout their lives.

5.   Not all patients can be helped with short-term counselling.

CHAPTER NINE

Assessment

The counsellor working in primary care should think of him/herself as an apprentice with each new referral, where he/she is learning from the patient in order to facilitate them in their journey.

As stressed earlier in the text, a thorough assessment is often key to the successful outcome of counselling in primary care. This assessment may begin before the person enters the consulting room, as the counsellor may glean useful information from the GP's referral letter.

Burton (1998) suggests a set of inclusion criteria for brief therapy. Her first suggestion is that the patient must also be suitable for long-term counselling or psychotherapy:

- can respond to an interpretive approach;
- is able to work in the transference;
- has sufficient ego strength—no risk of ego diffusion or disintegration;
- no history of gross acting out, such as repeated suicide attempts or life-endangering behaviour;
- not currently heavily dependent on drugs or alcohol;

- no active psychosis or part psychotic episodes;
- no severe borderline personally disorders without psychiatric backup (Burton, 1998).

Her second suggestion is the importance of a focus being found with the patient; third, that there must be circumscribed pathology, and fourth, the patient must be involved in object relations; in other words, this not for someone who deliberately isolates themselves from others.

However, what Burton presents above is the ideal. Experience has shown that most people who present for counselling in the surgery will not fit neatly into the above criteria. This does not mean that they cannot be helped by input with the counsellor. What it does mean is that the counsellor must learn to be flexible in their approach and be prepared to use the skills they have, be they psychodynamic, CBT, or eclectic.

This chapter is divided into three sections:

- assessment from a psychodynamic approach;
- assessment from a CBT approach;
- issues common to both.

Section 1
Psychodynamic assessment:
making a psychodynamic formulation

Gathering information, recognizing and assessing central conflicts

Making a psychodynamic formulation is a process that takes place during counselling, but particularly in the assessment session. As the counsellor listens to the patient's story and presenting problem, he/she attempts to formulate a link between significant relationships and central conflicts in the patient's past history and his/her present relationships. Additional clues and links may be made as the counsellor observes and experiences how the patient is relating to him/her during the session. The counsellor can often recognize embryonic signs of conflicts and problems that might arise in the counselling relationship (Mann, 1973).

Burton (1998) gives us an example of a psychodynamic formulation that is presented back to the patient:

> Given the pattern of physical and emotional abuse in your family, you came to expect that this was how you would be treated, so it was not surprising that you chose as a partner a man who would physically and emotionally abuse you. Now in therapy you expect that I will abuse you. [p. 64]

Malan's model, the triangle of insight (Figure 2), is useful in helping the counsellor and patient understand some of how they are feeling and why they behave as they do (Malan, 1976).

Burton (1998) explains Malan's triangle of insight thus: the current conflict is the precipitating factor that has motivated the patient to seek counselling, and the nuclear conflict is inferred from previous precipitating events, early traumatic experiences, or repetitive interactional patterns. Put together, the current conflict and the nuclear conflict comprise the focal issue in brief psychodynamic counselling or psychotherapy.

At this stage, it may be possible to assess a person's capacity for insight, self-awareness, and ability to make links between events and emotions from the past with the present.

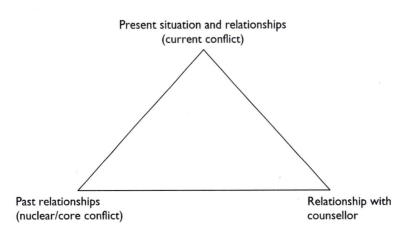

Present situation and relationships
(current conflict)

Past relationships
(nuclear/core conflict)

Relationship with
counsellor

Figure 2. The triangle of insight (Malan, 1976).

Recording information: the patient's present life and past history

To write up your psychodynamic formulation as depicted by the triangle of insight in Figure 2, above, three important areas need to be attended to:

1. Sketch in words the dynamic factors that appear to explain the current situation in the patient's life in the present.
2. Make a hypothesis about the formative influence of the patient's early experiences on the current predicament.
3. Predict the likely impact of these factors on the counselling being offered in the primary care setting.

To make a decision about whether brief psychodynamic focused counselling is appropriate, the counsellor must also take into consideration other information, as stated below.

Recognizing and assessing mechanisms of defence

The primitive defence mechanisms are those of splitting, idealisation, devaluation, introjection, denial, projection, projective identification, and regression.

The more mature defence mechanisms are repression, reaction formation, undoing, displacement, emotional isolation, intellectualization, rationalization, and sublimation.

Mechanisms of defence are unconscious psychic processes that are normal and essential for personal survival. We use them to help us remain intact as we meet and negotiate our developmental milestones and life's normal difficulties. However, these defences can become unhelpful and destructive when they are employed excessively and inappropriately in normal, adult, everyday relationships and situations. A person may become emotionally "stuck" at a level of development where the "primitive" defence mechanisms were needed for survival, but are not needed in such an entrenched form in their adult life. It must be borne in mind while carrying out the assessment in the first session that a person will be anxious and regressed, to a greater or lesser degree, when entering this new counselling setting and experience. Regression is a primitive defence mechanism, and in this state we often employ other primitive defence mechanisms. The counsellor must gauge whether these are entrenched and potentially destructive or limiting, or whether they are due to anxiety about beginning the new experience of counselling.

Defence against instinctual impulses, manifesting itself as resistance

It is recognized in the counselling profession that all people have an unconscious life and processes which house, well out of view from the rest of the world, our instinctual impulses that affect, if not govern, our lives and behaviour. In primary care counselling, we are not in a position to analyse these impulses, but we must recognize that they are active. Within the counselling contract and frame, the mechanism of defence set up by a person's ego will begin to feel threatened, and the person will deploy resistance to this phenomenon. This is called active resistance to uncovering what the person does not wish to have uncovered, for example, murderous impulses. For instance, when a patient feels that some painful material is about to be uncovered, he/she may start to come late or stop coming for counselling altogether, or he/she may develop some other symptom as a distraction.

There are many possible forms of resistance. In addition to the ego resistances, there are the transference resistances, which are differently constituted and are not usually used in short-term counselling.

Defence against affects (emotions)

Affects associated with the instinctual impulses that arise within interpersonal relationships, such as love, longing, jealousy, mortification, pain, mourning, hatred, anger, and rage will also be defended against, both in the counselling room and in outside life. It is often these impulses, which are "breaking through" a person's defences, causing symptoms, that bring the patient into counselling. A person has only a limited number of possible means of defence at any one time and in any one situation. People deploy different defences according to the stage of their life or the situation in which they find themselves.

These defences show themselves in the patient's behaviour as:

- repression;
- regression;
- denial;
- rationalization;
- projection;
- projective identification;
- displacement and reversal, etc.

For example, in rationalization, a person will attempt to rely upon reasoning or intellectualization rather than succumb to displaying emotion.

In short-term psychodynamic counselling, it is often possible to facilitate softening of these defences by gentle means in order that the person's life becomes more bearable or liveable. However, it is not our job to break through defences unless we have good evidence that the person has a strong ego and support network and it is what they wish to happen.

Permanent defence phenomena

These are body or personality traits which are obvious for all to see: for example, bodily attitudes such as stiffness and rigidity, personal peculiarities such as a fixed smile, contemptuous, ironical, and arrogant behaviour—all these are residues of very vigorous defensive processes in the past, which have become dissociated from their original situation (conflicts with instincts or affects) and have developed into permanent character traits (Freud, A. 1993).

These are mentioned here merely to inform the primary care counsellor, rather than to suggest they may be changed by a short-term contract.

Case study 1. Terry: a short-term psychodynamic contract

This patient presented as very jolly and jokey with good ego strength and a strong support network (supportive wife, employment, and several close friends) and was able to make use of short-term counselling with its three important components of brief dynamic counselling, these being: early confrontation of the resistance, high activity on the part of the counsellor, and the counsellor's overall attitude in brief therapy that is, keeping the end always in sight and part of the work throughout (Molnos, 1995).

Case history

Terry lived with his wife and small son, and his wife was now expecting twins. They had a good relationship and were able to spend a lot of time together, as Terry's current employment was four nights a week working as a locum GP. He had completed a carpentry course, and enjoyed being with his six-year-old son making furniture in his workshop at home. However, now, with two more children on the way, he and his wife realized this almost idyllic life would come to an end, as Terry would soon need to earn a lot more money and they would need a bigger house.

Terry's mother, aged fifty-nine, had been dependent on prescription drugs for thirty years and Terry had decided to train as a doctor after his father died suddenly, aged forty-nine, as a result of a diabetic coma. Terry was then twenty-four when he began his training. His older brother was already a GP, and had been asthmatic since childhood. Terry said he had always been very close to his Dad, and they were "soul mates". As Terry described his relationship with his father, the counsellor became aware of the pressure his father had put upon Terry to achieve and how much he wanted him to be a doctor like his older brother. Terry said he told his father everything and they always enjoyed making things together. Terry had decided at age six that he wanted to be a carpenter or a doctor when he grew up, and had been in training for carpentry when his father died. Terry was shocked by his father's sudden death and began to feel guilty at going against him by taking up carpentry as a career. He decided then to train as a doctor and, after his marriage, Terry's new wife supported them both financially for several years while he was training.

When Terry presented for counselling he was stressed by the need to soon begin to earn considerably more money. He said he was on a "knife-edge of stress" and had developed irritable bowel syndrome. He loved his carpentry, but this brought in little or no profit. He admitted that sometimes he felt bored with life. When he had qualified as a doctor he had joined a group practice and loved the buzz and excitement and thought that perhaps he was addicted to change and challenging situations. However, he said he reached "burn-out" after five years, probably because he tended to become too emotionally involved with his patients. It was at this point, when his wife was expecting their first child, that he decided to leave the practice and complete his carpentry training to become a cabinet-maker, using his locum work to earn enough money to live on.

Psychodynamic formulation

Terry appeared to see the counselling as an exciting challenge. He seemed confident and told the counsellor that his friends, when he told them he was coming for counselling, said they felt sorry for the counsellor because he would "be very challenging" for her. It soon transpired that this jolly, jokey stance was a defence against feelings of not "matching up", which perhaps reflected his relationship with his father. Also his wife, although supportive in many ways, had very good personal reasons for making it very clear to Terry that, with three children, she expected him to knuckle down and do a "proper job".

Session one

"I can tell you're not going to be a pushover," said Terry at the beginning of this session, after the counsellor had set the contract and boundaries of the six-session contract.

"Perhaps that is somewhat of a relief for you?" she reflected to him.

"Yes and no," Terry said, giving a boyish grin. "Yes, it's a relief because I know I have some soul-searching to do, but no, it's not a relief because I rely a lot on my power of getting the better of people and getting my own way—not my wife though, she sees straight through me."

"Perhaps that is why you married her," observed the counsellor.

Terry then attempted to engage the counsellor in religious and philosophical debate. She handed this back in a challenge about perhaps not wishing to engage with her or his inner emotional life when the time they could spend together was so short, mentioning when they would come to the end in August. This evoked the reply, "That is what I tried to do with Dad in my teens—I wanted him to find me interesting after I had decided to become a carpenter and not a doctor." His eyes filled with tears: "Any mention of my Dad and him not being around now goes 'ping' inside of me. I thought at the beginning I would only need a couple of sessions to make a decision about my future, but now I realize I will need more if my emotions are going to be involved."

Session two

The counsellor was beginning to realize that all Terry's "roads" (past conflicts and present avoidance of emotion) led to his relationship with his father. She tentatively made the link that perhaps becoming a GP would have pleased his father, and that in doing so he may have been trying to make some kind of reparation for choosing to be a carpenter against his father's wishes. Also, that this need to make reparation was present again in his life with his wife and children and their need for a financially secure life. If he chose to return to a GP practice, an old inner conflict may be resurrected, although this decision may serve his need for challenge and some possibility of excitement. Terry filled with tears again, and the counsellor was able to look with him at the possibility of an underlying depression. This exploration resulted in Terry realizing that he had a belief that if he did not force himself to work really hard, he might do nothing at all, and that would mean he was a failure.

Session three

Terry returned in this session saying that what he had discovered about himself in the last session had been a revelation to him. He had not realized how much effort he had to exert to maintain a status quo in his emotional life. He had come to realize that he did everything to excess, eat, love, and play. He said he even did to excess being a daddy to his son, but was always left feeling he needed more.

"Perhaps that 'more' that you are left wanting is your own daddy's unconditional love and approval," the counsellor mooted.

There was a long silence where Terry struggled tearfully with this observation. As he sobbed, he came painfully to see that he was never going to attain his father's unconditional approval, as he was dead, and that perhaps his strong faith in his God and Father was linked to this need.

"Maybe one of the things you got from being a GP was that you could be a 'father' to your patients and that is why you so often became so emotionally involved with them," reflected the counsellor.

"Maybe," he replied with a tinge of anger in his voice.

"Perhaps you looked for love and approval from them too?" the counsellor ventured.

Another silence, but this time Terry's anger was more apparent, as he then clenched his fists and said, "You're so bloody right, aren't you?"

His anger at the counsellor coincided with a month's break in the counselling, due to his annual holiday and then the counsellor's.

Session four

Terry said how glad he was to come after what had seemed an interminable length of time. He described how he had spent a whole month wondering whether the counsellor would be angry with him for his "outburst", as he put it, at the end of his last session. Terry also described how the effect of this ensuing inner turmoil had been on his relationship with his family. He felt he had taken his anger out on his wife and son—he felt desperately ashamed at his behaviour and did not want to behave like that again.

"You went into your break wondering what my reaction would be to your standing up to me in that way. Perhaps you believed at some level I might disappear like your father did, or that I might feel rejecting towards you?"

"Yes I think I did—it certainly put me in turmoil for a whole month," he said, again with a tinge of anger.

The counsellor then confronted Terry with "Perhaps you have come today wondering whether having counselling is such a good idea for you if it has this devastating effect?"

"Well, it hasn't solved any of my problems, has it?"

"Perhaps the revelation you spoke of a month ago feels less valuable than you thought, or perhaps the month without my support felt devastating?"

Terry lowered his head and cried silently for some time.

"This is the end of our fourth session, but I will be here for you for the next and the final session if you want to come," the counsellor stated at the end of the session as Terry left.

Session five

The counsellor reminded Terry that this was their penultimate session, and she surmised that, as he had attended, perhaps he was showing his desire to complete his contract with her.

"Yes, but I need you to know that I don't like you making me feel angry with you so often," Terry put into the space.

"I can understand that Terry, but I think you feel you still have some unfinished business here," suggested the counsellor.

"I am still not sure whether to go back to being a GP in a practice and risk having to move away from our friends or do something entirely different."

"You put that statement as if it is an either/or situation. Could there be other options?" asked the counsellor.

"Like what? Terry replied.

"Are you saying you cannot think of any other options and you want me to tell you?"

"Well, that would be nice," Terry replied, again with his boyish grin.

"The reality is that no one can make this decision for you," stated the counsellor.

Then came a long silence.

" I'm so afraid I will get to our last session next week without having made a decision."

"And how would that make you feel?"

"Pretty pissed off actually, since that's what I came for," Terry said angrily.

"If that is why you came how come you didn't look at your options with me earlier in the six weeks?"

"Now you're tying me up in knots!" Again, said angrily.

"That is a hard place to finish today," the counsellor concluded.

"Yes."

Terry then sat in silence to the end of the session.

Session six

Terry looked a little sheepish as he entered for this session.

"When I cooled off last week—which took several days by the way—I told my wife about where I've got to in my counselling. How I was at the end and still hadn't made a decision about my career path. I got very upset."

Terry went on to tell the counsellor how supportive his wife had been about this and that he was surprised by her response to his needs—that she wanted to help him make that decision. They had looked at some different options and explored honestly their individual feelings about them. It seemed that Terry was beginning to see his wife as someone he could relate to as an adult—he realized that up until now she either seemed like a pressuring parent (like his father) or someone to be looked after, rather weak and dependent upon him (like his mother).

The counsellor interpreted that maybe his relationship with her in counselling had given him a very different experience of being with a woman, and perhaps that had been enough for him to begin a more adult-to-adult relationship with his wife. That he was now in a better position emotionally to see himself in a different light, as an adult, not someone continually at the mercy of either always needing other people's approval and unconditional love or having to be continually the one in control and being "a father to all".

This seemed a better position for Terry to be in to face the rest of his life and decisions about his and his family's future.

As he left, he said, "Well, it's goodbye, but don't you go thinking I've finished with you yet." Although he said this in a jokey manner, the counsellor felt that perhaps one of the points he was making by this remark was that he had internalized their relationship enough to make use of it in the future for himself.

*   *   *

The next case study is an example of a patient being referred to a psychodynamic primary care counsellor for a short-term contract in which she could be held and contained through a crisis (suicidal ideation and threatened suicide). The counsellor's additional brief was to assess the patient for possible longer-term counselling.

Case study 2: Betty, referred by her GP and visiting consultant psychiatrist

Betty, a married woman aged forty-four, was taken to their GP by her husband because she had been depressed for some time and was now threatening suicide. The reason she gave to her GP for not consulting him sooner was that if he knew how ill she was he would sign her off work. Betty told the GP that her work as a neo-natal nurse with sick newborn babies was her lifeline, and that she would "go mad" if she had to stay at home all the time.

Dr John, her GP, insisted that she have two weeks off work while she began taking an antidepressant. She agreed. However, Betty had an unusual reaction to the antidepressant, resulting in dizziness, vomiting, and slurring of her speech. This frightened Betty and her husband and family, and she became unable to function with everyday tasks.

A consultant psychiatrist regularly visited the practice, and Betty's GP managed to get Betty to see him. He prescribed a different antidepressant and suggested she begin counselling with the surgery counsellor in three weeks time, to which she reluctantly agreed.

Case history

Betty's natural mother was unable to keep her at birth for reasons unknown to Betty. She was placed in a children's home for eight months before being adopted into a family with one other adopted daughter, aged three. Betty's adoptive family were a middle-class family who were able to give their daughters the "normal" things, such as presents at birthdays and Christmas, dancing lessons, and a stable home-life. However, Betty grew up experiencing herself as second best and that her older sister was the "blue-eyed" child, with Betty always coming second in her adoptive parents eyes. When Betty was six, her parents had a child naturally, a boy who literally had blue eyes, and who was "adored by my parents", according to Betty. She told the counsellor that her adolescence had been filled with teenage angst about not being popular or good at anything.

Betty's present relationship with her husband appeared to be a very dependent and possessive one, and her relationships with her parents, siblings, and her own two children were very difficult as they constantly seemed to be letting her down or being awkward. The counsellor kept to herself her own opinion that Betty needed people around her to "dance to her tune" and not display needs or personalities of their own.

During the assessment, while asking the normal questions to gain a history to Betty's current situation, the counsellor experienced Betty as quite withholding and regressed in her way of answering; she seemed very self-conscious, embarrassed, and often monosyllabic. Towards the end of the assessment session, Betty voluntarily intimated that there was something she could never tell anyone. The counsellor likened the session to "trying to pull teeth", and felt that the six-session contract to which Betty had reluctantly agreed would be continually under threat of Betty not attending, although she noted that Betty had dropped in that she had something important and significant to tell. The counsellor was left wondering whether Betty would come for her first session in a week's time, as she could not commit herself to saying she would definitely attend.

However, with the relatively scant information gleaned, the counsellor was able to make the following psychodynamic formulation.

Psychodynamic formulation

The counsellor was able to make clear links between Betty's past and present relationships. She experienced several features of Betty's relationships being played out in the counsellor–client relationship during the assessment session.

Betty's rejection by her birth mother (and father, who was never mentioned) and the subsequent six months she spent in a home before adoption had left Betty with an inadequately integrated inner world. Being in a situation where she was unable to make a secure attachment with one care-giver left her emotionally disabled, vulnerable, and reliant upon her early defence mechanisms of projection and splitting. Betty needed these mechanisms in order to survive and cope in her subsequent life and relationships. However loving and constant her adoptive parents may have been, they could not compensate for the utter desolation, separation anxiety, and aloneness that Betty carried with her into her adoptive family.

Betty almost certainly attempted to ameliorate her inner loneliness and desolation first by becoming a neo-natal nurse (using her strong identification with these very vulnerable babies) and then by her choice of partner, who possibly needed someone to be totally dependent upon him (for his own reasons). Her own two children, having left their babyhood needs and ways behind, became separate people, which Betty found almost intolerable. The more her children found their own identities and the more her husband became a workaholic, the more depressed and clinging Betty became. Once married, Betty experienced her adoptive parents as uncaring and neglectful, not only of her and her husband, but of her offspring (perhaps seen as continuations of herself).

Betty's way of relating to the surgery counsellor in the assessment indicated her dislike of other women, her mistrust in relationships of any kind, and her seeming almost to will the counsellor to reject her by being dismissive and withholding.

First session

> Betty did attend her first session, saying her husband made her come, but she remained silent for most of the fifty minutes. When the counsellor attempted to reflect with Betty upon the silence by saying, "Perhaps it is quite difficult for you to know where to begin today," Betty shrugged her shoulders in a dismissive way, all the time looking down at the floor and slightly turning away from the counsellor's gaze.
>
> "Perhaps you feel somewhat exposed in here today with me," was another attempt made by the counsellor to make empathic contact with Betty. To this, Betty replied, "I'm not bothered."
>
> The counsellor tried again after another silence, "Maybe you feel anything you might say here would not be right or of interest to me." This seemed have an effect on Betty, as she turned further away and

lowered her head almost to her chest. Again at the end of the session the counsellor said she would like to see her next week, and again Betty would not commit herself.

Second session

Betty entered saying she was only there because her husband had brought her. After a few more attempts at some contact made by the counsellor, Betty began to cry silently. Her tears dripped off her nose on to her clothes and she made no attempt to mop them, but she began to sniff loudly—the counsellor felt they seemed almost aggressive in nature.

"I wonder if it is difficult for you to talk to me today because I am not asking you questions—it is very different from our first assessment session."

"Yes," Betty mumbled into her chest.

"Are there some questions you would like me to ask you, Betty?" Somehow, by calling Betty by her first name in this way, the counsellor had unlocked the floodgates and Betty began to sob loudly and uncontrollably as she said angrily, "I don't know." At which point, Betty stood up and left the session early. On reflection, the counsellor felt that Betty perhaps had been angry at being "found out" and "found wanting".

Third session

By this time the counsellor was really beginning to feel Betty's inner pain and rage. Betty had managed to communicate through the unconscious mechanism of projective identification (the unconscious process of projecting elements of the psyche into another's unconscious and enlisting the other person's identification with them) just how much she needed to have her inner pain and conflict held and contained, but also how angry and vulnerable her possible dependency upon this person (the counsellor) would make her. The counsellor was beginning to realize how intolerable this was becoming for Betty.

"This is very difficult for you, isn't it, Betty?"

"I don't know if I can do it," stated Betty, "and there is something I can't tell anyone."

"You don't know if you can keep coming but there is something you need to tell?" asked the counsellor.

"I don't know".

At this point, the counsellor reflected to Betty that telling was going to be difficult and that perhaps she could just say what was the most difficult thing about telling it.

"It's stupid," replied Betty.

"Perhaps you think you will feel stupid saying it."

"Well, it's not very nice," Betty replied forcefully.

During the remainder of this session, the counsellor stayed working in the same vein as above with Betty's resistance to disclosing, gently teasing out why it would be so difficult to tell. The counsellor said that she understood that Betty might feel stupid, but that she did not see her as stupid in any way.

Session four

In Betty's fourth session some basic trust seemed to have been established between her and her counsellor, because she disclosed that, at age seven, she had been sexually abused by "a man on a bike", who was "friendly" towards her as she walked home from school one day. He gave her sweets and then "cuddled" her. She said he had not hurt her. Knowing how vulnerable Betty would have been, the counsellor wondered (to herself) whether she had actually quite enjoyed the affection and attention, perhaps felt special in some way. The counsellor knew intuitively not to reflect this to Betty.

When Betty returned home for tea and told her mother about the friendly man, "all hell broke loose", as she put it. She said her mother "marched" her down to the local police station where she was "made" to give a statement to a lady police officer in a room without her mother. It became clear to Betty's counsellor that it was probably the negative attention and hue and cry surrounding the ensuing investigation that traumatized the seven-year-old Betty more than the "abuse".

Session five

Betty did not attend the fifth session, but made a suicide attempt serious enough to put her in hospital overnight, frightening her husband, family, and counsellor. It seemed that "having" to tell her counsellor about the abuse brought back all the feelings of shame and judgement that she experienced as a child. Her consultant psychiatrist visited Betty in hospital, where she told him that she would not see the counsellor again because she was too intrusive and judgemental. The psychiatrist knew this to be untrue of the counsellor, whom he regularly supervised in the surgery. The psychiatrist called a meeting with the counsellor and the GP after Betty agreed that they could discuss her further treatment in her absence. After reviewing the case so far, which, of course, predated Betty's counselling in the surgery, it was felt that as she had only one more session left of her surgery contract, and as her relationship with her counsellor had engendered such devastating feelings of shame, rejection, and anger, that a different, longer-term form of therapy might prove more manageable for Betty. The counsellor was distraught, feeling she had failed Betty, but was subsequently able to see that this was another unconscious communication from Betty. Betty continually felt a failure and wanted her counsellor to feel the same way, perhaps to triumph over her in some way, as she may have wanted to triumph over her birth mother. Perhaps, too, she needed to feel less impotent in her life and relationships.

Betty eventually agreed to see an NHS CBT therapist, who was part of the Community Mental Health Team, for an assessment. She found being with a man and having a more structured, cognitive approach suited her better, and she was able to stay with this therapist for several years, in which time a relationship slowly built in which Betty could trust.

Section 2
The CBT approach

Any event in a person's life has special meaning, which is idiosyncratic to them; it is a matter of individual interpretation. Therefore, for a counsellor to understand a person's distress, they must understand the person's individual way of perceiving events in their world. CBT attempts to reduce distress by helping people to change their cognitions. Beck puts it thus: cognitive therapy is "an active, directive, time limited, structured approach . . . based on an underlying rationale that an individual's affect and behaviour are largely determined by the way in which he structures his world . . ."

(Beck, Rush, Shaw, & Emery, 1979, p. 3). A person in distress may have, for example, a core belief that they are unlovable and defective in some way. This can lead to dysfunctional assumptions about people and relationships resulting in negative automatic thoughts (NATS) about themselves. Negative automatic thoughts are involuntary, situation-specific, and often plausible, and they overlay underlying assumptions, such as "people will find me boring", and core beliefs, such as "I am unlovable". In CBT counselling, the counsellor challenges these negative thoughts early in the work. In the case of depression, a person often has an excessively negative view (core belief) of the world, the self, and their future. Core beliefs are not generally tackled in short-term counselling.

Cognitive assumptions—individual interpretations of events—affect behaviour. Helping a person change what they do can change their systems of thought and feeling. In CBT, a person is helped to break the cycle of cognition (thoughts, beliefs, etc.), affect (emotional states), physiology (bodily states), and behaviour (what one does or says).

The idea of CBT counselling being a collaborative project for both counsellor and patient is an important place to start the work. Knowledge and goals are shared and it is understood that the patient is an authority on his/her own problems, but the counsellor brings the expertise that enables possible ways of looking at those problems.

The aim of the counselling contract is to change the mutually agreed focal problem. The patient's history is important in the formulation, but in short-term CBT counselling the here and now is the focus. Focusing on the here and now problems may often result in thoughts and feelings about the past being mitigated.

CBT is a "scientific" approach using behavioural "experiments" with the patient. It is structured and active. The counsellor and patient set an agenda, which helps to structure the sessions and keep the focus in sight at all times. The type of structure depends upon the patient's personality type (e.g., autonomous *vs.* dependent), and can vary according to patient feedback.

Assessment, formulation, and developing a treatment plan

Detailed assessment is needed in order to implement a CBT formulation for treatment. The CBT model, therefore, becomes individualized, which requires the taking of detailed information about the patient's experiences and symptoms. Clarifying the current problem is important for focusing on the vicious circles of thoughts, feelings, and behaviour, which maintain the problem in the person' life.

Formulation is important, because it acts as a bridge between CBT theory and individual experience.

The benefits of a good formulation (Mueller & Riggs, 2008) are that it:

- acts as a bridge between CBT theory and individual experience;
- makes seemingly chaotic and unpredictable events more understandable;
- reduces client's (and therapist's) confusion and demoralization;
- may begin to shift patient's negative explanations of problems;
- provides a shared rationale for developing and agreeing treatment plans;
- helps understand (or even predict) difficulties in therapy and / or therapeutic relationship.

The process of assessing a person's current problem is not just about gathering facts. It also involves gathering information on a person's thoughts, body states, behaviour, and mood states. This process helps to break down and simplify complex problems. It can give some hints about possible maintenance processes. Then a tentative hypothesis can be made about what might be the reasons for the person's pattern of problems.

Making a formulation

Diagrams are often useful when making a formulation with a patient. Counsellor and patient will be looking for the "vicious circles" of behaviour and thought that might maintain the problem (see Case Study 3, below, for Shelley's CBT formulation).

Some common maintenance cycles

- Avoidance of situations or escaping as soon as possible.

- Reduction of activity: limiting one's life, which avoids the "problem" situation but also limits enjoyment.
- Safety behaviours: when there is fear of some disaster, the person does something they believe will prevent the disaster happening, and when the disaster does not occur, the person believes it was the safety behaviour that stopped it.
- Catastrophic misinterpretations: feelings of anxiety lead to a panic attack, which is seen as a life-threatening illness, which leads to increased anxiety.
- Self-fulfilling prophecies: negative beliefs in relationships, which lead to withdrawal from people or hostile behaviour, which, in turn, leads to other people ceasing to try to make contact, which then confirms the belief.
- Hyper-vigilance: worrying about getting ill, which leads to continual checking of perceived symptoms, which leads to ordinary bodily sensation being misinterpreted, which leads to worry and anxiety symptoms.
- Performance anxiety: the anxiety disrupts the performance through, for example, stuttering and shaking, which is a confirmation to the person of their poor ability to perform, which leads to worry.
- Perfectionism: setting unrealistically high standards of which a person falls short, which maintains the belief of inadequacy.
- Fear of fear: anxiety from any cause causes anxiety symptoms, such as fast heart rate, frequency in urination; these are experienced as very unpleasant or frightening, and the person then anticipates the fear, which leads to anxiety.
- Depression, which leads to low mood, which leads to negative automatic thoughts.

Assessment for short-term CBT uses a Socratic method of questioning, a dialogue requiring a gentle and curious stance. It was a method Socrates used during the latter part of his life as he concentrated upon logic and ethics.

Talking about Socrates, Plato said,

> He set himself to accomplish his divine mission by systematic questioning, in the course of which he not only cleared his opponents' minds of much muddle and misconception, but developed his own

two important contributions to logic, namely adduction and general definition. [Plato, 1983, p. 10]

When a particular concept came up in conversation, Socrates would question his opponent in a way that gently but logically teased out the meaning of that concept with which they could both agree or disagree. In other words, the result of the conversation was that the two people could adduce meaning from a certain word or concept. This type of questioning is used to open up different views for the patient to consider.

Cognitive–behavioural therapy has traditionally focused mainly upon the relief of symptoms. It has been used to treat anxiety, obsessions, compulsions, phobias, and post traumatic stress disorder. Some patients are naturally drawn to a method that will relieve symptoms and have, for whatever reason, little interest in exploring the underlying intrapsychic or historical causes of their problems. People who fall into this category will often choose CBT if it is offered, or drugs to relieve their distress. I stress here that the experienced CBT therapist will still need to set the present problem in the context of the patient's past history and continue, during treatment, to be informed by that knowledge.

Assessment of behaviour focuses on the target behaviour in terms of its antecedents and consequences. Burton names this as the A-B-C model (Burton, 1998). In other words, it asks what triggers the "problem" behaviour, and asks what are its consequences. It is believed that negative automatic thoughts can be important in initiating and maintaining "problem" behaviours. The word problem is in inverted commas because, as I have mentioned earlier, it can be argued that the "problem" may be seated not in the person identified as the patient, but elsewhere. Also, problem behaviours may mean behaviours that are problems to someone else!

Gathering information, recognizing and assessing core beliefs

During the assessment, the CBT therapist will be looking for links between thoughts, behaviours, and feelings while listening to the patient's story. He/she will be trying to uncover the person's core belief system about themselves, other people, and the world. The counsellor will be assessing how these beliefs affect thoughts, feeling, and behaviour.

Recording information

Some therapists find it useful to use charts and diagrams for record-ing the information that the therapist and patient have uncovered and understood together. This shared written information can then be compared with later progress information gathered during, and at the end of, treatment. It is important that the patient is helped to become an equal partner in the work.

Behavioural assessment

There needs to be a detailed description of:

- the presenting problem;
- other problem areas;
- the patient's skills;
- pleasures and positive characteristics;
- the development of problems and previous coping attempts;
- expectations of treatment.

Functional analysis

This is carried out on the presenting problem giving attention to:

- behaviour and cognitions: antecedents producing increase or decrease in symptoms;
- background factors producing increase or decrease in symp-toms;
- consequences of the behaviour, both positive and negative, on the patient and significant others;
- thoughts, images, and behaviours that are incompatible with the problem behaviour. [France & Robson, 1997, pp. 26–27]

Behavioural interventions

Burton (1998) lists the common behavioural interventions as:

- reinforcement;
- modelling;
- shaping;

- response cost (the loss of positive reinforcement for certain behaviours);
- time-out;
- differential reinforcement of other behaviour;
- stimulus control;
- exposure;
- systematic desensitization;
- contingency contracts;
- assertion and social skills training;
- homework;
- investigation into the likely effect of change on the patient and significant others.

Burton (*ibid.*) believes that the principle of reinforcement underpins much behavioural therapy, that is, reinforcing adaptive behaviours and ignoring or extinguishing maladaptive behaviours.

Control of the patient's environment is another important behavioural principle, for example, rearranging the environment so that triggers to certain behaviours are eliminated. This may take the form of moving to a different area; for example, moving away from parental control or changing place of employment.

Homework

Homework, consisting of exercises, written or behavioural, that the patient performs and practises at home, is common in CBT therapy. It is, thus, important to assess a patient's motivation in the assessment interview. However, motivation or a lack of it soon becomes apparent as the sessions go on.

Burton (*ibid.*) asserts that perhaps the most widely practised form of CBT in primary care today is Beck, Rush, Shaw, and Emery's (1979) cognitive therapy for depression. CBT can address negative automatic thoughts and avoidant behaviours, and these changes, in turn, will positively affect depressed feelings. The cognitive model of depression acknowledges the importance of early experience of loss, criticism, or rejection from parents, leading to the formation of dysfunctional assumptions, for example, "unless I'm loved, I'm worthless".

It is my experience that CBT for moderate to severe depression has a better outcome if it is practised over a period longer than six sessions. People suffering moderate to severe depression have to contend with unpleasant symptoms of their "illness" that often have the effect of making them wish to withdraw from normal activities and relationships. These symptoms (for example, self-denigration, guilt, self-loathing, low self-esteem, sleep and eating disorders) can leave the person feeling isolated and worthless. Longer-term CBT, as with longer-term psychodynamic counselling, uses the relationship between counsellor and client as an important tool in recovery. All the elements of growing trust, validation of feelings, affirmation, emotional containment and holding have the opportunity to facilitate the person to greater integration and understanding of the reasons for their depression.

Computerized three-session anxiety management

Computerized three-session anxiety management programmes have been installed in some GP surgeries to be used by patients with mild disorders, eliminating the need for a therapist. This method is now part of the stepped-care approach to treatment used in the new IAPT (Improving Access to Psychological Therapies) Pathway initiatives in operation in some parts of the country. Patients need to be selected carefully for this form of treatment, as the therapeutic elements of the relationship between patient and counsellor will be missing. For many people, it is the therapeutic relationship that facilitates motivation to carry out the therapy. However, for people who find relationships with others very difficult, or who are highly cerebral and rely heavily upon their cognitive abilities, this may be a good choice.

Phobias

Some people suffering from a phobia can be helped with the six counselling session CBT model adopted by most GP surgeries, using a gentle introduction to the principles of desensitization, in a safe, holding environment with the possibility of referring on for longer therapy either through the mental health services or privately. Some GPs may sanction a longer-term contract for certain patients who find it very difficult to access treatment outside of the surgery.

Case study 3. Shelley: short-term CBT contract (assessment plus six fifty-minute sessions)

Shelley, aged thirty, was referred by her GP to the surgery counsellor for an assessment of her phobia around being stuck in heavy traffic, which she had suffered with for eighteen months. Shelley recounted that because she was suffering panics and loose bowels when travelling more than about a two-mile radius from her home, she had left her employment as salesperson with a well-known brand of beauty products. She had loved her job and it had been a big promotion for her. She was now back to being a self-employed beautician in a local beauty parlour that barely paid a living wage. The GP had enquired if she had ever had a road accident or a bad experience when waiting in traffic in the past, and she replied that she had not.

Case history

Shelley had moved to the south of England four years previously, leaving all her family in Wales, and her phobia began about one year after moving to set up home with her boyfriend. Shelley said she and her boyfriend were happy together, and she saw it as a long-term relationship leading to starting a family at some point. She could make no connection between the move and the phobia, except that it was very difficult now for her to visit her family on her own because of her fear of traffic hold-ups. Before training as a beauty therapist, she had been a talented lady cricket player, and had been in the Cardiff junior ladies' cricket team. Due to a back injury, she did not make it into the adult team.

Assessment

The counsellor and Shelley first looked at her symptoms. When Shelley was stuck in stationary or slow moving traffic, she would begin to become very anxious; her right arm would begin to tremble, her heart would race, and a pain would begin to radiate from the centre of her chest, which she thought could be a heart attack. If the traffic did not start moving within a few minutes, she became worried that she would need the toilet, not be able to reach one, and then wet or soil herself in the car. If she was a passenger in the car, the symptoms would be less intense but still around. Consequently, she and her boyfriend had stopped going out unless it was very local to their home. Shelley feared he would get tired of this restrictive life and leave her, although there were no indications that this was going to happen.

After extensive exploration of Shelley's past, she and the counsellor could uncover no precipitating factors for the phobia. The counsellor gently observed that she felt Shelley was dealing with the phobia by avoidance of these troubling situations and that part of the their work together would be facing her fears and gradually exposing herself to longer drives. With the help of the counsellor, Shelley could learn to manage her feelings. The counsellor felt that the situation Shelley had arrived at was one of fear of her fear, and that they would move through a pro-gramme using worksheets together in the sessions. Shelley would continue to monitor and record her thoughts, behaviour, and feelings between sessions as she gradually exposed herself to traffic and longer drives. Shelley agreed to this and to the six-week contract.

Session one: case conceptualization and formulation

At the beginning of this session, the counsellor was confronted with a very angry Shelley. Although in the assessment she had seemed to accept what the counsellor had suggested as the treatment plan, that is, gradual exposure and monitoring of symptoms, Shelley expressed anger and disappointment at the counsellor not being able to fix the situation quickly. The counsellor responded with empathy and under-standing, and asked Shelley if she would just look with her at what she could offer to help and then make a decision about continuing. Shelley agreed, and they began to fill in the daily thought record (see Table 1, pp. 134–135). Shelley understood what she would need to do with the daily thought record in the week between her sessions.

Session two

Shelley returned to see her counsellor having recorded a small success. She and her boyfriend (G) had visited friends six miles away in the next village, and she had driven home. While they were visiting their friends' house, G had twisted his left ankle, which would make it painful changing gear. G said he really needed her to drive home, and with the encouragement of G and their friends, Shelley faced the challenge with courage. The counsellor talked over carefully with Shelley her entries into her daily thought record and was able to encourage Shelley to carry on with counselling.

In the second half of this session, the counsellor introduced a new chart, consisting of a model for CBT formulation (see Figure 2) where the counsellor described to Shelley what a maintenance cycle was. This involves identifying maintenance processes, which are habitual thoughts and behaviours that perpetuate the phobia. The counsellor asked Shelley to consider what her maintenance processes were, which they identified as centring around safety behaviours, escape/avoidance, and reduction of activity, and to bring them back to the next session.

Session three

Shelley had not found the task an easy one, as just thinking about driving made her feel in a panic. The counsellor affirmed that Shelley had tried very hard and had faced her fear by doing the task. She said she thought her habitual safety behaviour was to divert her mind by phoning a friend whenever the thought of having to drive somewhere came into her head, instead of staying with her fearful thought. Shelly said that this behaviour was not working very well now, because her friends were getting a bit fed up with it.

Her avoidance behaviour had been to stop driving, and her reduction in activity had been to leave her job in sales, which took her far afield, and to work within walking distance of her home.

It became obvious that Shelley wanted the counsellor to feel her anger at how hard the task had been for her, as it was not until near the end of this session that Shelley told the counsellor she had driven to the shops, two miles away, using her identified alternative thought to her automatic thought (see Table 1, pp. 132–133). As a consequence, she

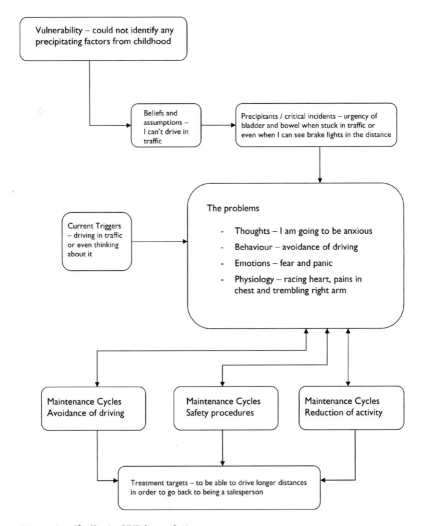

Figure 2.   Shelley's CBT formulation.

had felt much less anxious, knowing that whatever happened she could quickly return home for her toilet needs.

By the end of this session, Shelley was agreeable enough to take on the notion that, in the next session, they would design an experiment together to help her face her fear of fear.

The counsellor also gave Shelley a pamphlet on managing phobias. As their contract was going to be short, the counsellor felt the written information would help to consolidate work so far done together, and could serve to hold Shelley while she managed the intervening week.

Session four

Shelley came in saying the pamphlet had been very helpful, probably more helpful than the counselling! The counsellor sensed again some anger in this statement and reflected that counselling was much harder work and more challenging than Shelly had thought. Shelley agreed and asked why the counsellor had not given the pamphlet to her in the first session.

The counsellor asked Shelley to bear with her and look at carrying out the experiment. Together, they looked at what distance drive Shelley felt she could attempt that would challenge her safety behaviours, her avoidance, and her reduction in activities. Shelley decided the only way she could attempt it was to do it straight away after the session. She would walk straight home, get in the car, and drive to the nearest town, ten miles away, to buy some beauty products she needed from the wholesaler. This drive would involve some traffic, mainly stopping at traffic lights, and she would not phone a friend. Walking home, she would remind herself that the main problem for her was fear of her fear, as she had taken on board that this was the main source of her distress.

Session five

Shelley was very pleased she had managed the ten-mile drive and was able to wait to visit the toilet when she arrived at the wholesaler. She had managed the drive home well and did not even feel she needed the loo.

Shelley and the counsellor talked all of this over in great detail in order to reinforce the success in Shelley's mind and feelings. They filled in the experiment in the daily thought record.

Session six

In this session, Shelley recounted some more drives she had done, each time feeling less anxious beforehand. The counsellor felt it appropriate to speak to Shelley about how angry she had felt from time to time during the contract. They were able to tease out from this that Shelley's father had always had little patience with her when she was learning something new, like riding her bike, and that had probably resulted in being quite anxious about trying anything new. They pinpointed that the phobia had come on a few months after Shelly started her new job as a salesperson, and that perhaps it was her anxiety at starting something new rather than the driving that had caused her some considerable anxiety, and that perhaps she had unconsciously been able to deny this reality because she loved the new job.

After one month Shelley returned a very positive evaluation form for the counselling.

Section 3
Assessment of areas common to psychodynamic and CBT approaches

As counselling is a talking therapy, a person must be able to communicate in a way that understanding can pass between patient and counsellor. Look for the patient's ability to give a coherent narrative of events in their life.

For an effective outcome to short-term counselling, there needs to be some evidence that the person has the ability to make and sustain relationships, work (not necessarily paid), play, and look after themselves to some extent, and to have a personal support system in place.

Recognizing the symptoms of depression

GPs are very used to seeing the symptoms of depression, but occasionally, if there has been some time lapse between the GP suggesting counselling and the patient making an appointment with the counsellor, a person may have fallen into a depression in the intervening time. Some careful questioning is helpful for both the counsellor and patient to recognize whether they may be depressed. Ask the patient to look over the preceding two weeks and say if they have:

• felt sad or miserable most of the time;
• lost interest or pleasure in most of their usual activities;

Table 1. Shelley's evaluation form.

Situation or event	Feelings	Automatic thoughts (images) 1. What were your thoughts as you experienced the feelings. 2. Highlight the most powerful thought	Evidence which supports your most powerful thought	Evidence which does not support your most powerful thought	Alternative to your automatic thought. Write an alternative to your most powerful automatic thought and rate the degree to which you believe in it on a scale of 0–100	Describe how you are feeling now
30th July 2007 Getting stuck in traffic	Fear, nausea, panic, and racing heart	I am trapped, I will not be able to get to a loo and might wet or soil myself and have a heart attack. I see brake lights even when there are not any. The most powerful thought is that I will not get to a loo. I have an image of me sitting on a toilet	Within seconds of being stuck in traffic I suddenly feel an urgency to wee and sometimes have a loose bowel as soon as I get to where I am going	I have never wet or soiled myself in the car	I am well in control and if I do wet myself I can just drive home and sort myself out instead of going where I was going. On a scale of 0–100 I rate my belief as 5	I do not have much faith in this method and still feel very anxious

(continued)

Table 1. (continued).

Situation or event	Feelings	Automatic thoughts (images) 1. What were your thoughts as you experienced the feelings. 2. Highlight the most powerful thought	Evidence which supports your most powerful thought	Evidence which does not support your most powerful thought	Alternative to your automatic thought. Write an alternative to your most powerful automatic thought and rate the degree to which you believe in it on a scale of 0–100	Describe how you are feeling now
6th August 2007 Driving home, accompanied by boyfriend from friends 6 miles away	Fear and racing heart but no urgency to wee but did not get stuck in traffic	I am nervous and I expect I will get stuck in traffic at the main roundabout but if the worst comes to the worst G can take over even if it hurts his ankle because it's not broken. My most powerful thought is that I will be pleased to tell the counsellor about my success if I make it	I haven't been able to do this for ages	I have never wet or soiled myself in the car but if I do it won't be the end of the world	G and I are both in control and all I am suffering from is fear of my fear. I rate my belief as 25	I still don't have great faith in this method but I have a little more confidence in myself

- lost or gained weight or had a change of appetite;
- experienced sleep disturbance—either sleeping more or less than is normal for them;
- felt slowed down, restless, or excessively busy;
- felt tired or had no energy;
- felt worthless or excessively guilty;
- had poor concentration or been very indecisive;
- had recurrent thoughts of death.

Recognizing and assessing coping strategies

We all have coping strategies, but we are not always aware of what they are because mostly we apply them unconsciously. Counsellors, through their training and personal therapy, will perhaps be more aware than most people what their coping strategies are and how well they work in everyday life.

The counsellor must ask him/herself whether this is a person who will need help with reinforcing their coping strategies: for example, do they have little ego strength, are they in crisis, or are they recently bereaved?

It cannot be stressed enough how important coping strategies are to people in distress, whether that distress is occasional or chronic. In short-term and especially supportive counselling, our task as counsellors is not to abolish coping strategies that are working for the person, but, rather, to help the person first to recognize their useful strategies and then to facilitate the reinforcing of them. We may also help them to understand how some of their strategies are a hindrance rather than a benefit in their lives.

People use these coping strategies in different situations that challenge them or in order to cope with feelings that threaten to overwhelm. The patient that we see in the GP surgery will have his/her own unique set of coping strategies, which may or may not be known to them. Strategies such as having a drink to gain "Dutch courage", retail therapy, or going fishing when the going gets tough at home are those we all know. These are conscious strategies. Less obvious are the strategies that a person uses as safety measures, or that cause a person to habitually avoid certain situations, unaware that that is what they always do. It is these less obvious ones that may come to light during counselling and can be a revelation to the patient.

During the assessment session, the counsellor may feel that a patient is strong enough to be challenged on their strategies in order to help them develop and grow as a person, but, if in doubt, it is wisest to wait until later in the short-term contract.

Attitude towards, and ability to, change

Gentle questioning about any transitions and losses that have occurred during the patient's life will give clear indications of his/her ability to cope with change. It may also become clear, as the patient tells their story, whether they have the necessary motivation and capacity to make changes in their behaviour and attitudes. Some people can take on board the concept that it is easier to change yourself than try to change others.

Attitude towards authority and ability to work in partnership

A person's attitude towards authority figures often becomes clear during the assessment, perhaps as the person talks about his/her GP or parents. This attitude can help the counsellor assess the patient's ability to work in partnership as they attempt to enter into negotiation about the way forward. If the person has a mature attitude towards authority, that is, having respect without the need for rebellion or total compliance (childlike behaviour), the person will feel empowered by working in partnership with the counsellor and appreciate the ensuing feeling of mutual trust.

If the person has a childlike attitude to authority, working in partnership will take some time to establish, if at all. A childlike attitude would manifest itself in, for example, defensiveness, anger, and lack of co-operation or over compliance.

Values and goals

It is important to discover what is valuable to a person before trying to set goals, as we all value different things in life. Sometimes, we are led by another person's goals and values, which can put us at odds with ourselves. Through the assessment session, it is possible to ascertain whether the person normally has short-term or long-term goals, or has no goals at all.

Support network

We all need a support network within our lives. This may comprise supportive relationships and a certain structure to life. Each person has different needs; for some, having steady employment, income, and a spouse or the companionship of others in their leisure time provides the support they may need. It does not take a huge leap of the imagination to see how this support structure could easily be ruptured in today's social climate in this country. A person often presents for counselling because of marital or relationship break-down and loss of work, perhaps through redundancy. Assessing the patient's support network gives the counsellor an indication of how much challenge the person may withstand throughout the counselling. One would not, for instance, challenge someone's attitude to change when they have just been significantly bereaved.

It may also become clear, through the patient's story, that what looks like a good support network hides the fact that they may have a diminished ability to seek and use that support. We all need to ask for help sometimes! It is amazing how many people find it almost impossible to receive help even when it is offered.

The person may use their family or work colleagues for support, but have no idea how to elicit support from outside organizations, for example, the Citizens Advice Bureau, Social Services, a solicitor or the Job Centre. It is interesting that this inability to seek and use support ranges across all socio-economic circumstances.

Drugs, medication, their effect on the patient, and side effects

Illegal and prescribed drugs can cause changes in a person's thoughts, feelings, and behaviour. It is not only psychotropic drugs that can cause these changes. Medication prescribed for other physical conditions can also affect the person mentally as well as physically. For example, an under-active thyroid or antibiotics can make a person feel low in mood. It can take up to two years to hit on the right dosage of thyroxin for a person suffering from an under-active thyroid. The counsellor should try to gain knowledge from the patient about what drugs they are receiving, especially psychotropic drugs, and how they are affecting the person. When the counsellor is unsure about side effects, most GPs are helpful in this area when consulted. The next chapter looks at psychotropic drugs, their use, and side effects.

Knowledge of any physical illness

Acute or chronic illness can also cause changes in a person's mood, sleeping pattern, and ability to carry out normal everyday tasks. This alone can cause a reactive depression and/or anxiety. A recent diagnosis of cancer or other life-changing disease can have a devastating effect upon a person, and they may need time to integrate this knowledge into their psyche. Hyper-thyroidism can cause rapid heartbeat and an increased rate of metabolism. Before diagnosis, this could be confused with a panic attack, and sometimes the person's personality appears to change until the condition is treated satisfactorily. Therefore, it is important to rule out these causes before the counselling begins in order to have a whole picture of the patient's situation.

Somatization

Somatization occurs when a person's physical symptoms are manifestations of emotional disturbance. Examples of this can be headaches, backache, muscle tension, blurred vision—in fact, the list is endless, as each person who is prone to unconsciously somatizing their emotional pain has their own unique way of expressing it physically. It is often difficult for a GP to recognize the difference between somatization and organic illness. It takes time for physical tests to be carried out, thus it can be some time before the patient is referred to a counsellor. It is often difficult for the patient to accept that the pain they are suffering has an emotional cause.

Suicidal ideation

Many patients have suicidal thoughts. For many, it is a way of thinking about escape from a bad situation that appears to have no end. Many patients have also thought about how they may carry out their death. But not all of these are at risk of carrying it out. It is often the people who have not thought about it or talked about it with anyone that make a sudden attempt and succeed in killing themselves. The person most at risk is the person who has little or no personal support and lives an isolated life, although one can feel isolated in a marriage or a family. Unsuccessful suicide attempts are much more common, and are a cry for help or an angry response to not being heard or taken seriously.

Psychiatric history and history of drug or alcohol abuse

Gaining this knowledge from the patient fulfils two tasks. The first is to get a picture of possible mental illness or acting out in the past, or how the person deals with psychic pain. The second gives the counsellor clues to the patient's ability to give a coherent account of their life and how organized/disorganized their thinking is at present.

Neurosis and recognizing neurotic symptoms

I use the word neurosis here as a technical, descriptive term and not a pejorative one. I would never advocate calling a patient neurotic; it has too many negative connotations.

Laplanche and Pontalis (1988), in *The Language of Psychoanalysis*, define neurosis as "a psychogenic affection in which the symptoms are the symbolic expression of the psychical conflict whose origins lie in the subject's childhood history; these symptoms constitute compromises between wish and defence". They go on to say that "the extension of the term 'neurosis' has varied: it is now usually reserved, when unqualified, for those clinical pictures, which can be ascribed to obsessional neurosis, hysteria or phobic neurosis" (p. 266).

It must always be remembered that although counsellors are trained to recognize psychopathology, be it neurosis or psychosis, our aim is to help the whole person. Thus, it is always the person with whom we are forging a relationship and not divorcing their psychopathology from them so that we can treat "it". Neuroses are psychic responses to life, rooted in infancy and reinforced over time. Originally, they serve to shield or defend the individual from intolerable pain and conflict. Each person has his or her unique way of doing this to make life liveable. Perhaps the reason the person has come for counselling is because those neurotic functions are not working very well or have completely broken down. The person now needs to be heard so that their unhealthy responses can be understood by the counsellor, but, more importantly, understood by themselves, in order that new and perhaps healthier responses can begin to be put in place.

People presenting with unhelpful neuroses will come with depression, states of generalized anxiety and depression, panic disorder, phobias, and obsessive–compulsive disorder. These types of presenting problem are often seen in primary care, and are often treated with medication and counselling unless the individual does not want to begin on the route of medication. In this case, counselling alone would be offered, with a view to preparing them for longer-term counselling. The length of counselling will often depend on the severity and length of time the person has suffered with their symptoms.

The diagnosis of depression often covers a wide range of aetiology. Reactive depression is, as it says, a reaction to some event or illness: for instance, bereavement, loss of job, or a major change in a person's life.

Longer standing depression, which can begin in childhood and often in adolescence, can still be seen as a reaction, but to a major early trauma, physical, emotional, or mental abuse, or loss of self.

Also presented by patients in primary care are states of mind that, over time, would improve spontaneously. This may be anxiety in the face of a specific event or perceived difficulty that, once experienced, disappears. Depression and distress after an uncomplicated bereavement—by thism I mean when the person grieves appropriately and for a time—is considered within the bounds of normality. Other individuals become pathologically stuck in the grieving process and need counselling help to move on. Patients also present with sleeplessness and unexplained medical problems, which can cause considerable distress and can be helped greatly by a counsellor spending time listening to their distress and facilitating the person in finding solutions.

People with neurotic symptoms usually know that they are behaving irrationally or experiencing irrational thoughts and feelings. People suffering from psychosis are often unaware that they are ill and displaying irrational behaviour, because their behaviour makes sense to them.

The above is not an exhaustive list of the neuroses or of their aetiology, but I trust that a counsellor trained to diploma level will have covered this in their theory and clinical training. Below, I list some common symptoms that may be presented in primary care. For a more in-depth look at the neuroses, I recommend Anna Freud's *The Ego and the Mechanisms of Defence* (1993).

Neurotic symptoms

- Fear of social situations (social phobia), flying, and other phobic reactions.
- Intolerable anxiety, often related to Oedipal conflict issues.
- Invalidism, often rooted in a person's fear of separation and avoidance of independence.
- Perfectionism.
- Promiscuity.
- Alcohol and drug dependency.
- Pathologically low self-esteem not related to life changes.
- Inability to eat in public.
- Blushing.
- Self-deprecation.
- Inappropriate outbursts of anger.
- Sadomasochism, meticulous orderliness, and compulsive cleanliness of person or surroundings without underlying paranoia.
- Conversion reaction, that is, unconsciously converting psychic pain into physical pain.

It is worth remembering that the above symptoms may not be the ones that the patient presents to the GP, but are quickly revealed as troublesome in the assessment for either psychodynamic or CBT counselling.

The borderline patient

The word "borderline", in Rey's terms (Rey, 1979), refers not only to a category of patient, but also to a particular aspect of mental structure of these patients and to the location of the self in that structure. He describes the patient to feel him/herself to be neither fully inside nor fully outside their objects. They appear to exist in a borderline area that corresponds to what Steiner calls a psychic retreat (Steiner, 1993). In this psychic area, they are protected from anxiety but have problems with identity, so that they feel neither fully sane nor quite mad. These problems with identity can extend to their sexual maturity and expression, and may leave them in a state of feeling neither a child nor an adult, and neither loving nor hating. They live in a borderline between two conditions of being. The borderline patient often feels, consciously or unconsciously, that he/she has been prematurely removed from maternal care and space, and, thus, is forever in a state of trying to regain that place. This can manifest itself in primary care as a patient who is resentful, angry, intolerant, and very needy but who has little insight or capacity to change. Their stance in life is that everyone else in their life should change to accommodate them.

In borderline and psychotic patients, containment brings relief but does not necessarily lead to growth and development within the person's experiences of life. The individual's relief seems to last only while the containing counsellor or doctor has an ongoing presence in his/her life, as the capacity to contain cannot be internalized.

Recognizing and understanding personality disorders

Steiner's description of personality disorders is interesting; he calls them pathological organizations of the personality, because that is what they are. They are not the patient's fault and often cause a great deal of grief to the person and those around them (Steiner, 1993).

Steiner (*ibid.*) puts forward that it may be simpler to consider the whole literature on pathological organizations of the personality under the heading of "narcissistic organizations". He suggests this is because of the defensive or pathological splitting and projective identification that comprise this organization, which implies that a narcissistic type of object relation is involved. Steiner also suggests that Riviere (1936) was perhaps the first author who studied narcissistic object relations and emphasized the highly organized structure that results from the way objects and defence mechanisms are linked together.

Castillo (2003), in her book *Personality Disorder*, writes from a study carried out for and by service users with a personality disorder as defined in *DSM-IV* (*The Diagnostic and Statistical Manual of Mental Disorders* (American Psychiatric Association, 1994, p. 459):

> These are impulsive people who make recurrent suicide threats or attempts; affectively unstable, they often show intense inappropriate anger. They feel empty and bored and they frantically try to avoid abandonment. They feel uncertain about who they are and lack the ability to maintain interpersonal relationships.

Castillo quotes Lewis and Appleby: "Personality Disorder appears to be an enduring pejorative judgement, rather than a clinical diagnosis" (Lewis & Appleby, 1988, p. 44). It is this pejorative judgement that Castillo, in her study with patients, wished to mitigate by seeing and relating to them in a holistic and humane way. I highly recommend her book for anyone wishing to understand more about personality disorder and to experience her humane approach to these unhappy and damaged people.

The study of personality disorder is not the remit of this book, and there is not room to do the subject justice. However, it is my experience that someone who has been labelled as having a personality disorder will often fall into one of three categories: predominantly displaying dependent, aggressive, or paranoid behaviour and thought patterns. Because of their difficulties in relationships, they are prone to depression and anxiety and can be helped to some degree with supportive or CBT counselling. These often severely suffering people will need perhaps a six-week contract with a counsellor whenever their lives change or become less stable. These people are also more prone to eating disorders, self-harm, and have problems with their self-image. I say more about this in Chapter Four.

There are people in this category who may be considered to be a danger to others as well as to themselves, who are antisocial and dangerous to society. They are more likely to be known to the criminal justice system than seen as a patient in primary care.

David Fainman, of the Henderson Hospital, suggests that

> behind the label of personality disorder there is a personality, behind which is a person. We have struggled with what these labels mean for years. All of us have personalities and ten per cent of us in the general population are considered to have a personality disorder. [Tyrer & Stein, 1993, p. 42]

Beck has more recently turned his attention to CBT for personality disorders (Beck et al., 1990). This is one of the few therapies that will attempt to treat personality disorders and would not be suitable for short-term therapy in a GP surgery. Beck and colleagues (*ibid.*) assert that a chain of cognitions, perhaps in the vein of "they don't like me", will often lead to core schema, that is, the person habitually responds to life and relationships as if they are not liked or, in many cases, not loved. "Schema relate to central and basic organising systems for knowledge about the self and others. These are built up through life as the result of interpersonal experiences" (Gilbert, 2000). This can lead to the person feeling unlovable. There may be more than one core schema, and, thus, the therapy may continue long-term.

Recognizing when the presenting problem is primarily a social one

Many patients suffer very difficult social situations. Poor housing conditions or lack of suitable housing for their situation can be at the root of a patient's great distress and symptoms. In our society in Britain today, people expect to have separate housing for different generations of the same family and to have it at an affordable price. Most people expect to be fully employed or, if not, that the benefit system will provide enough for more than just basic survival. When these expectations are not met, problems can arise. The gap between the rich and the poor, even in this country, is widening, and, thus, more expectations are being left unrealized.

When a patient presents themselves with depression and/or anxiety, it is often that they are frustrated, angry, and feel let down. If the person is a lone parent, even with family support, unresolved past issues can rear their head. For example, a young, single mother may wish to live separately from her parents and is housed in a small flat or bed-sit. She then becomes torn between her need to be independent and her often crippling loneliness and lack of freedom. A counsellor may witness this scenario many times, and see their task as counsellor not just to hear her pain, but also to facilitate her in making changes in her social structures to make life more bearable.

Debt and loss of income through redundancy or unemployment is another area that can cause mental and emotional suffering. It is not enough to point out to someone where they have gone wrong in their decision making. The patient may have found him/herself in that situation through attempting to fill an emotional gap by resorting to "retail therapy". This, in turn, may be a social solution learned from the nuclear family. A mixture of psychodynamic understanding and a CBT approach can, for some, be very helpful in a short-term contract.

People in the above situations can become distraught and unable to cope, which can cause an emotional breakdown. However, this can be recovered from quickly once it has been recognized for what it is, and a combination of practical as well as emotional support provided. Again, a mixture of a CBT approach with some psychodynamic understanding can go a long way to being helpful.

The above is not an exhaustive list of the type of social problem being presented in the counselling room and, obviously, there will be patients who are either so distressed or mentally and/or emotionally unstable that they cannot make use of what is on offer. This type of patient may need some medication and/or social work intervention before they are able to make use of counselling.

Ethnic minorities

People belonging to an ethnic minority often suffer social depriva-
tion, especially in some areas of the country. If English is not their
first language, they may need an interpreter when they present for
counselling. The NHS nationally employs interpreters to help in
this situation. These patients are likely to be low-paid and in poor
housing.

Assessing capacity for insight, self-awareness, and ability to link present to past experiences

It is not only psychodynamic counsellors who use the patient's
capacity for insight and the ability to link past to present; the CBT
counsellor will value knowledge of a person's history in making
formulations about core beliefs that have their roots in childhood.

A trial interpretation may be made in the assessment, but sometimes a patient's need to tell their story may have to come before
assessment of insight and self-awareness. Having said that, an
experienced counsellor can unobtrusively gain an idea of a person's
capacity in this area as the person tells their story.

For a person to have insight and self-awareness, they need to be
able to conceptualize the presence of an inner world, their world of
internal processes unique to them and its connection with the outer
world. For many, it is an alien idea that we, as individuals, are not
only reacting to, or orchestrating, the outer world, but we also have
an inside world that has its part to play in decision making and
behaviour. For some, it is an easy leap of the imagination to understand and take on board this notion, but for others it seems impossible. For other individuals, an assessment plus six sessions can be
enough for them to become encouraged in this way of thinking and
find that the resulting insights help them see a way out of their
immediate problems. These are often people who have shown the
ability in the assessment to link past situations and relationships
with present ones. For instance, when Jack came for a counselling
assessment, he had already made the link for himself between the
feelings he was experiencing since his wife left him and all the feelings of abandonment and anger he had when his mother left the

family home when Jack was fourteen. Not all patients are able to make the link for themselves, but can do so with help from the counsellor. Not that this is the entire answer to their problems, but it can help the person to begin to understand the strength of their emotions.

Assessing a client's support network

The reason for assessing a person's support network is so that you can gauge to what extent you may be able to challenge them or gently help them to a greater grasp of the reality of their situation or illness. You can never be certain how emotionally strong a person is from the first assessment session. Sometimes, you will be able to gain some idea of their ego strength from the GP's referral letter, but this may be sketchy about such matters.

People's support networks can vary greatly. We must not assume that what we might consider to be a good support system (e.g., supportive family, friends, and colleagues) will be the same for our patients. However, that area is a good place to start when asking questions about a person's life. You may discover that they derive more support from the local pub or church than from their family. For some, the work or college environment may be a their main area of support, and so the loss of employment can mean much more than just loss of income. For highly dependent people, the primary care environment can be a lifeline. For young people, their social peer group, gang, or sports alliances can be very important and supportive.

Through carefully selected questions, you will soon discover if a person is isolated and poorly supported, and also how much of a problem this is to them. Social isolation is not a problem for everyone, although most people require a minimum amount of positive social interaction. For some, even negative interaction is better than nothing.

Ability to seek and use support

Some people may appear to be well supported in terms of the number of people in their lives, but this can belie the true situation.

The person may be pathologically unable to ask for help or use the support that is offered. Another individual, who has always been considered strong and who copes with everything, may feel ashamed to ask for help. Or, with this type of personality, there may be a time lag between them needing and asking for help and support and their loved ones noticing and taking this seriously. It is not uncommon to see a woman who finds herself in this category in the primary care setting. With counselling, she can begin to see the reality of her situation and find a voice loud enough to make a difference, often very successfully.

There are people who have managed well in life but now find themselves, either through old age or illness, less able to manage and who need help to think in terms of what is out there in the community that they may be able to tap into for assistance. Others merely need encouragement to do what they know is right for them.

There are still elderly people in our society who are fiercely independent and are not aware of financial benefits open to them. I am not suggesting counsellors become social workers, but merely facilitate the person's confidence and ability to deal more effectively with what is so distressing in their lives.

Key issues

1. Thorough assessment is a key factor in successful short-term counselling.
2. Attitude to change can affect successful outcome.
3. Coping strategies need to be understood and worked with.
4. The strength of a person's support network and their ability to use it may determine how much challenge they can tolerate.
5. Always check a person's physical state (other diagnosed illness), as this can affect their mental state.
6. Do not avoid investigation of suicidal ideation.
7. Remember that alcohol, illegal and prescribed drugs can affect a person's mental state.
8. Sometimes, the person's presenting problem is a response to intolerable social conditions.

CHAPTER TEN

Use of psychotropic drugs, their probable impact upon counselling, and their side effects

This chapter is taken from the BACP information sheet P8, 2005, written by Rachel Freeth, which she produced to provide an introduction to psychopharmacology for counsellors, psychotherapists, supervisors, and trainers (Freeth, 2005). I have included additional information supplied by the Depression Alliance.

Drugs are often prescribed with the same broad aim as counselling and psychotherapy, that is, to improve psychological functioning. The primary care counsellor will come across patients who are taking drugs, and this may be a concern to counsellors who are new to working in a healthcare context. It is useful, therefore, to have some knowledge about psychotropic drugs, including why they might be prescribed and their potential benefits and harm, and possible side effects that may affect the emotions or normal everyday functioning.

What is psychopharmacology?

This is the name given to the scientific study of the chemical receptors to which psychoactive substances bind, of the levels of these substances that are achieved in the brain, and of their effect on psychological functioning.

Why are psychotropic drugs prescribed?

These drugs are prescribed in response to symptoms, in the absence of a specific diagnosis or naming of a mental illness. It has, in some quarters, become controversial to speak of disease and illness for psychological and psychiatric problems. There are no scientific tests that prove the existence of mental illness, and this has led some to dismiss the biological model of mental illness because diagnoses within psychiatry are descriptive terms rather than representing concrete physical pathology. Diagnosis of mental illness is made on the basis of a person's mental state and their individual description of their experience, both of which are subjective. Also, many doctors and psychiatrists are aware of the stigma attached to diagnostic labels, and this can lead to an ambivalence of diagnosis.

Patients often see the physical symptoms as the problems that need treatment. For example, difficulty in sleeping, "butterflies" in the stomach, reduced appetite, or general irritability are often symptoms that are taken to the GP for treatment. In psychiatry, symptoms also include experiences or mental phenomena that an observer would consider abnormal, but which may not seem abnormal or distressing to the patient. Difficulty in sleeping may occur in a depressive illness or in an anxiety disorder. Delusional beliefs can occur in schizophrenia and in bipolar affective disorder. Hence, psychotropic drugs are prescribed, in order to tackle symptoms rather than a specific diagnosis, and the rationale for a psychotropic drug being prescribed should never be assumed. For instance, lithium, which may be prescribed for a bipolar disorder, can be used as a mood stabilizer for severe depression (see Table 2).

When should the counsellor consult with a doctor regarding a patient's medication?

Some patients are confused about why and for what purpose a certain drug has been prescribed. The GP or psychiatrist may not give adequate explanations about why the person is on a specific drug, or what its side effects are. If a patient withdraws too quickly from a drug, for whatever reason, and without consulting their doctor, the withdrawal symptoms can seem worse than the symptoms the drug was prescribed for in the first place. With the patient's consent, a counsellor may wish to consult with the doctor for further information, or the counsellor may suggest the patient consults with their doctor to help them feel less confused.

Major categories of psychotropic drugs

Table 2 gives information on the main categories of psychotropic drugs that the patient in counselling may be prescribed.

How psychotropic drugs work

Drugs change the pattern of brain activity by altering brain chemistry. The chemicals that comprise psychotropic drugs target receptors in the brain to increase or decrease the amount of neurotransmitter (normal brain chemicals) at the nerve ending. To date, it has not been proved that just because drugs alter the levels of neurotransmitter, it must be a deficiency or excess of these chemicals that causes the illness. Simply, the association is noted and a biological process is considered more to be a link in the chain of what causes mental illness.

The primary care counsellor will have his/her own ideas about what is most beneficial for any one patient, or patients in general, who exhibit psychologically distressing symptoms. This may influence how they approach counselling them. With growing experience of both patients and the diagnosing and treatment styles of doctors within any given practice, the counsellor will become skilled at "reading between the lines" of certain decisions made about patients. For example, Dr A may always prescribe antidepressants and only consider counselling if the patient does not respond well to that treatment, whereas Dr B suggests both at the same time. Dr C, however, may prefer to try a short course of sleeping tablets and/or tranquillizers when a person is displaying

Table 2.   Major categories of psychotropic drugs.

Class	Uses	Common side-effects
Anti-psychotics (neuroletics 1. Typicals—older drugs e.g., chlorpromazine (Largactil), trifluoperazine (Stelazine), haloperidol (Haldol). 2. Atypicals—newer generation with wider range of action e.g., olanzepine (Zyprexa), risperidone (Risperdal), quetiapine (Seroquel), clozapine (Clozaril). Some anti-psychotics are prescribed as an injection taken every one to four weeks	Psychotic experience and illness such as schizophrenia, psychotic depression, manic–depressive illness (bipolar affective disorder), especially manic phase. Also prescribed for the treatment of anxiety disorders in the absence of psychosis and as a short-term treatment for acute agitation.	Different types have different side effects. Newer drugs generally have fewer troublesome side effects than older types, which may cause Parkinson-like features, tremor, stiffness and involuntary movements. Other side effects include sedation, gastro-intestinal disturbances, dry mouth, weight gain, endocrine disturbances and blood disorder.
Antidepressants 1. Tricyclics—older generation e.g., amitryptiline (Tryptizol), dothiepin (Prothiaden). 2. SSRIs—Selective Serotonin Reuptake Inhibitors e.g. fluoxetine (Prozac), paroxetine (Seroxat), sertraline (Lustral), citalopram (Cipramil). 3. SNRIs—Serotonin and Noradrenaline Reuptake Inhibitors e.g., Venlafaxine (Efexor), Mitrazepine	Mainly prescribed for depressive illness and anxiety disorders but also for obsessive–compulsive disorders, eating disorders and chronic physical pain.	Gastro-intestinal disturbances (nausea, constipation), urinary retention, dry mouth, blurred vision, sedation, cardiovascular effects and sexual disturbance, SSRIs can also cause agitation and aggression.

(*continued*)

Table 2. (continued).

Class	Uses	Common side-effects
Anxiolytics The main class is benzodiazepines e.g., Diazepam (Valium), lorazepam, temazepam, nitrazepam (Mogadon)	To relieve anxiety and/ or induce sleep. Commonly used for the severe agitation of psychotic states and acutely disturbed behaviour or severe acute emotional distress. Also used in the management of alcohol withdrawal and epilepsy.	Main disadvantage is dependence. Side-effects include headache, confusion, blurred vision, and gastro-intestinal disturbances.
Noradrenaline Reuptake Inhibitors (NARIs) e.g., Reboxetine (Edronax)	This antidepressant works by increasing levels of noradrenaline in the brain.	Feeling dizzy or faint when you stand up, constipation, dry mouth, insomnia, feeling hot and sticky, especially at night.
Mono Amine Oxidase Inhibitors (MAOIs) e.g., Isocarboxazid (Marplan), Phenelzine (Nardil), Tranylcypromine (Parnate) Reversible Inhibitors of Monoamine Oxidase-A (RIMAs) e.g., Moclobemide, (Manerix)	These antidepressants work by blocking an enzyme called Monoamine Oxidase. The MAOIs have been around for about 30 years and are effective for all types of depression, including depression with unusual symptoms and depression where other antidepressants have not worked well.	Feeling dizzy or faint when you stand up, feeling sleepy in the daytime, constipation, dry mouth.

anxiety with depression, and to see if a spell off work helps before considering other treatment.

If a patient's thought processes and emotions appear to be significantly affected by psychoactive substances, a counsellor may question the usefulness or validity of the therapeutic counselling process at the present time for that patient.

The impact of acute and chronic illness on emotions and mental functioning

This section looks at some of the physical illnesses that can cause psychological disturbances and symptoms for which psychotropic drugs may be prescribed in addition to the medication for the physical illness. Brain disease, such as epilepsy or tumours, comes into this category. Endocrinal diseases, such as an underactive thyroid gland, can induce depression and an overactive gland can result in feelings of increased anxiety. Other endocrinal disturbance and hormone imbalance can leave a person feeling confused and often irrational.

A person can have a reactive depression after a bout of flu or other dramatic, though relatively short illness, including post-surgery. Undiagnosed diabetes can cause tiredness and lack of energy plus other changes in metabolism, which may eventually take a person to see their GP. Once diagnosed, the person may have difficulties in coming to terms with the diagnosis and organizing their lives when having to self medicate (e.g., insulin injections several times per day). The person may have an angry or depressed reaction. If the person cannot or will not take good care of himself/herself, hypoglycaemia (a deficiency of glucose in the bloodstream) may result, which, due to the effect of inducing sometimes erratic emotions and behaviour ("going hypo"), can cause problems in interpersonal relationships.

Organic disease such as a brain tumour, or brain abnormality such as epilepsy, can affect a patient's emotional life. Degenerative eye disease or any degenerative disease, such as multiple sclerosis, will also affect emotional life and interpersonal relationships.

Amputation, hysterectomy, or mastectomy can leave a lasting reaction, which, if misunderstood, can cause problems for the person. Stroke or chronic fatigue syndrome can result in a person becoming emotionally labile. Chronic pain can affect the brain, as the "body map" of the affected part (i.e., the part of the brain which houses the mental representation of that body part) increases in size. Chronic pain can often cause the person to feel isolated and can cause depression.

Useful further reading: British National Formulary, Pharmaceutical Press. This should be available to the counsellor within the primary care setting. It is regularly updated.

Useful websites: www.nmhct.nhs/pharmacy, provided by Norfolk Mental Health Care NHS Trust.

Key issues

1. GPs are usually willing to discuss prescribed drugs and their effects with the counsellor.
2. Some acute and chronic illnesses have an impact upon emotions and mental functioning.

CHAPTER ELEVEN

The contract

Within the primary care setting, the largest percentage of referrals for counselling present as depression and/or anxiety. If the GP writes a referral letter, he/she will normally state the symptoms that the patient has presented in consultation. As the counsellor becomes more experienced and begins to be able to read between the lines of doctors' referral letters, he/she may be able to glean what is underlying those symptoms. GPs develop styles of referring that can give many encoded clues.

Some symptoms of depression and anxiety are normal reactions for any person when something is experienced as "at odds", out of balance, or confusing, either physically or emotionally, in their life. At this point, due to our dependence upon the NHS in our society, it is quite usual to consult with our GP as our first port of call when we feel unwell in a way that is not normal or manageable for us. Also, most GPs who employ a counsellor within the primary care setting will tend to refer anyone who requests counselling to that counsellor rather than to an outside agency or private practitioner.

When a trainee is on his/her clinical placement, his/her mentor or a more experienced counsellor within the setting may have screened the patients that they are allocated to counsel. It is important that this screening takes place in order that a trainee works within their competency. Unfortunately, not all mentors offer this service.

Frame issues

The frame is the boundaried setting of counselling. No frame within the counselling contract is totally without impingements from the outside world and, in the primary care setting, the frame is likely to be more permeable than those found in counselling agencies or in private practice. In a GP surgery, there are many possibilities for the frame to be breached, for instance, when a receptionist gives the counsellor information about a patient other than that they have arrived for their appointment. Another example of this is when a GP stops the counsellor in the corridor to "helpfully" add to what he/she has already been told by the patient. On some occasions, a GP may refer two members of the same family for counselling to the same counsellor. If the two people have different surnames, this may not come to light until the patient begins to tell their story. Langs (1993) calls this the "permeable frame". Procedures for dealing with this kind of situation need to be thought about before it happens. If there are two counsellors working in the surgery, this difficult situation can be easily remedied by one counsellor seeing one patient and the other counsellor seeing the other family member. Firm boundaries within the setting can minimize contamination of the contractual frame.

Setting the contract

Counselling within the primary care setting puts the counsellor in the front line; that is, they are required to see everyone who is referred for an assessment. The counsellor will have to "think on their feet" and work creatively and flexibly. However, this does mot mean that setting the contract should be compromised.

As with counselling in other settings, a contract (usually verbal) is agreed upon by both patient and counsellor. Often, in the primary care setting, this contract is assessment plus six fifty-minute weekly sessions. Some PCTs have a contract that allows the counsellor to deviate from this norm at their discretion. Some instances of this are given later in this chapter. Some GPs will require the counsellor to carry out an assessment only in the first instance. This is to determine the patient's counselling or therapy needs so that the counsellor can then make recommendations back to the GP for either short-term help within the surgery, longer-term counselling, either within NHS secondary healthcare or private counselling in an agency, or a referral to a psychiatrist for a psychiatric assessment. When the doctors in a surgery favour assessment only, it may be possible for more appropriate counselling to be carried out, as only patients who fit the criteria for a good outcome are offered counselling. These patients would receive an assessment plus six fifty-minute consecutive counselling sessions taking place at the same time and on the same day each week. The contract would have a clear beginning, middle, and end. This continuity of contact works well, and it is worth taking the necessary time to forge the contract, taking an attitude of partnership with the patient.

At the time of making a contract, the usual contractual issues are discussed between counsellor and patient, for example,

- boundaries of time and space (when, where and for how long);
- confidentiality;
- managing DNAs;
- time-keeping;
- acting out and acting in, etc.

Normally, the counsellor working in the primary care setting will not be charging a fee directly to the patient. For many counsellors this will be an unfamiliar way of working, and he/she will need to find ways in which to help the patient value what is being offered.

The above would be considered good practice. However, in reality, when patients know that six free counselling sessions are available in the surgery, they are keen to receive their six sessions after assessment in order to "give that a try first" before investigating a different route, perhaps one which the counsellor and GP may feel is more appropriate for that person.

When the contract may deviate from the norm

Crisis counselling

Many people present themselves in crisis in the primary care setting, and these patients often find themselves put forward as an urgent referral for counselling. It is not appropriate to attempt in this situation to lead the person into finding a focus for a short-term contract. The person will almost certainly be emotionally labile and have irrational thought processes. The counsellor's task in this instance may well be simply to find a focus for each session. This needs to done after the patient has had time to relate their story and express their feelings about this within the holding frame of the first session. The focus could be looking at how the person is going to manage their life in the week between sessions.

Example of crisis counselling

A man is referred for counselling seven days after his wife has asked him to leave and he is sleeping on a friend's floor. He is likely to be angry, anxious, insecure, physically affected, and regressed. History taking may have to wait or be left to emerge over time. However, some structure in the shape of contractual boundaries and a focus for the week will be holding and reassuring. The man may have suicidal thoughts and/or a complete lack of normal functioning. The focus for this first session could be exploring with the person how they might find more suitable accommodation, how they are going to function at work, and whether it is necessary for them to be signed off sick by their GP.

Emergency situation

An emergency situation can arise if a patient comes in for her first session and is obviously severely clinically depressed/anxious/suicidal and unable to function. She tells you that her GP suggested counselling some time ago, but she has waited until she is highly distressed before taking up counselling. It is impossible to do an assessment because she is not able to give any coherent account of what is going on for her. You ask her about her medication: she was prescribed antidepressants a month ago, but stopped taking them because they were not helping. In this situation, the counsellor is in a very good position, working in the primary care setting, to implement an appointment with the doctor immediately, insisting she must be seen before she leaves the surgery. With the patient's permission, the counsellor is able to speak to a doctor to give an opinion on the patient and arrange an immediate consultation for emergency medication or intervention by a mental health crisis team. Discretion in this situation is called for, as some GPs like to feel they are in charge and do not appreciate the counsellor "interfering". However, it is my experience that in a situation like the above, GPs are only too ready to help and view the short-term resolution of the situation as teamwork.

Single session counselling with an "open door" approach

Christopher Cameron (2007) has researched this single session approach and published his findings in the BACP research publication *CPR* (*Counselling and Psychotherapy Research*). He refers to Bloom's findings (Bloom, 2001). He says it is tremendously important to clarify that single session psychotherapy (or counselling) is not just a condensed version of traditional psychotherapy. Maintaining an "open door" approach to some clients leads to optimal long-term outcomes. This idea can fit well with primary care counselling, since the surgery setting already has an "open door" policy for most of the population of this country. The "open door" counselling approach acknowledges that some patients will require additional counselling support in the future, if they experience further difficulties. When a single session has been helpful, the counsellor using this approach can then assume that patients can recognize their needs and, with well-timed help, can solve their own problems (Cambell, 1999). Counsellors and therapists can strive to create readiness for change and encourage patients to use what they found helpful in the session to achieve change (Talmon, 1990). Cambell believes that simply offering advice to the patient, reframing their problem, or normalizing what they perceive to be abnormal or unusual is often all that is required. Advice (a dirty word in counselling) given in the primary care setting is often exactly what is needed. A word of caution here is that the advice needs to be that which the patient feels they have arrived at for themselves and actually all the counsellor has done is to affirm those ideas.

Extended assessment

A GP may refer a person for an extended assessment if he/she is unsure whether the patient needs to be referred for a psychiatric assessment. This is by no means a regular occurrence and a trainee counsellor would not be expected to carry out this assessment. The counsellor would negotiate a six-session assessment period and report back to the GP when it was completed or before that if necessary. The patient would be informed that the GP has requested this assessment in order to make a suitable referral for the help that is most appropriate for the person. The counsellor will be looking for pockets of psychotic thinking, signs of borderline personality disorder, and/or bipolar elements of a moderate to severe depression.

When there is an impending court appearance

Waiting for an impending court appearance can be stressful and frustrating. A patient may be awaiting divorce proceedings or may have been accused of the abuse of a vulnerable person. Once an accusation of abuse of a child or other vulnerable person has been made, the person concerned is suspended from work immediately and often feels that they are being treated as if they were guilty before the trial or investigation. This can feel like an intolerable situation for the person involved, and they are well served by a six-week counselling contract with additional sessions perhaps spread out until the court hearing is over. This can serve as support for the person, as well as working through the issues involved in the situation.

When the patient is a witness

It is important that the counsellor seek advice when counselling someone who is due to appear in court as a witness. The Crown Prosecution Service and BACP, in partnership with Sage Publishing, have produced information on this topic (Bond & Sandhu, 2005; Home Office, 2002).

Legal reasons for counselling

There may be other reasons for receiving counselling that are connected to the legal system, for instance, as part of bail conditions. This could be a useful referral where the person makes good use of the sessions to look at him/herself, their life, and more appropriate lifestyle or life choices. For example, a young man who came as part of his bail conditions also worked well on some unresolved grief issues. However, he found organizing himself to come for sessions difficult, and did not attend his contracted six sessions.

On the other hand, the person may just be going through the motions of coming for counselling in order to achieve compliance with conditions.

Serious situations of loss, for example, miscarriage, still-birth, and cot death

Counselling someone following one of the above situations is probably the saddest and yet the most rewarding of short-term counselling contracts. However, it is probably a time when the counsellor must call upon his/her inner strength and be the most flexible of his/her career. Grief is an emotion that we all know and can identify with. We need strong internal boundaries, because it is in this high state of emotion that we are most in danger of merging with our clients and of projecting our own feelings and responses on to the other person. In this situation, there can be a blurring of who is the counsellor and who is the patient, and the counsellor may need to take extra care of him/herself at this time.

Miscarriage

The reader must never underestimate the loss caused by miscarriage. When a woman has lost a baby it is natural for her to grieve. However, to those around the mother at this time, a miscarriage does not seem as devastating as losing a full-term baby and the mother may feel hurried in her grieving process, or the need for it may not be acknowledged at all. This outside influence can be so strong that the mother may try to deny her need to grieve and, in this instance, there can be a long delay before the mother presents for counselling, as she may not want to burden others with her grief. There can be family pressure to look forward to the next baby. Sometimes, it is not until the first anniversary of either the miscarriage or of the date when the baby would have been born that a patient (this may be the father or mother, or both) begins to feel distressed, especially if there was insufficient grieving at the time. The person may consult their doctor with any number of symptoms that they do not link with the death of their child. Remember, too, that grandparents also grieve, especially if it is the first grandchild that is miscarried.

Still-birth

What many people do not know is that when a baby dies in the womb after a certain length of gestation, the mother must give birth to that dead child. She must endure the pain and often indignity of childbirth without the joyful outcome at the end of it. Even in this enlightened age, some would have the mother not see the baby or hold it, believing that she will not have a bond with it and that not seeing it will make things easier. This is where most counsellors must call upon their sense of empathy, as, unlike a lot of situations, he/she will almost certainly not have had first-hand experience of this devastating loss.

In the cases of still-birth, it is most likely that the mother, father, and other siblings will have already formed a relationship with the unborn baby, especially the mother. The child will have been felt and its movements seen, and often its small life will have been mapped and spoken off well before it is born. Imagine that sense of loss.

Cot death

This, I believe, is the most tragic of all deaths to bear. A cherished baby boy or girl suddenly is no more. It is difficult to write about.

Example: Carol

I think one of the most rewarding and touching times for me, as a counsellor, was when a young mother who had suffered a cot death came for counselling. The death had been ten years before, and she and her husband had then gone on to have two healthy, normal children. Ten years on, she was able to grieve her dead baby boy in my company. When he had died, the farming family into which she had married wanted and expected her to stoically bear the loss and look to the future, which is exactly what she did. In farming, birth and death of animals can be a daily event, and something to be moved on from. I found it interesting that it was a gynaecological problem and associated marital problems that were presented as the reason for needing help.

*　*　*

It is likely that a GP will refer a woman who has recently miscarried, had a still-birth, or a baby suddenly die because he/she knows the person will be grieving, but it is the counsellor and the patient who must decide whether this is the right time for counselling. The first stage of grief is numbness or denial, and when a woman and her family are in this place they may not be ready to continue on the path of grieving. This is where flexibility becomes the name of the game, and the co-operation of the patient is sought in order to make the best use of the counselling on offer. It may well be the first time that the patient is given a choice of "treatment" and it is important that she feels she really does have the choice of counselling now or later, or at any time of her choosing. For instance, in the case of cot death and perhaps after the first assessment session, it may be agreed that she return for more counselling after the funeral, or at least have a session at that time to "touch base" with her counsellor for security and containment. It must also be remembered that people grieve differently, and that this is not always a man–woman divide, although some stereotypical behaviour may have to be overcome initially. This difference in grieving or timing of grieving can cause rifts between couples and families, and in the primary care setting there is the unique opportunity to hold and contain the situation with more than one member of the primary care team becoming involved with the same family while confidentiality is maintained.

Pre and post termination counselling

All of the above, or none of it, can apply to pre and post termination counselling. For some patients, the decision to terminate a pregnancy seems to be an easy one. However, I have never ceased to be amazed at how far reaching that decision can be and how the accompanying emotions may be successfully denied for perhaps decades. It is a feature of the young, especially adolescents, to live for the moment. I believe they need this defence mechanism in order to do the internal work necessary to separate from their family. And it is often the emotions evoked by these early terminations that can lie dormant and surface at a later date to disrupt a person's equilibrium when they are faced with another emotional conflict or loss.

Example: Sandra

Sandra was referred to me for counselling after she had suffered two early miscarriages and had become inordinately distressed by them. Her husband and family were at their wits' end knowing how to help her, as she was healthy and no medical reason was found why this may have happened or why she should not go on to have a normal pregnancy. She told me of the termination she had undergone when she was fifteen, after she became pregnant by a boy at school of whom her family disapproved. In the second session, she owned that she had not wanted to have a termination, but her family had pressured her, and she had harboured guilt about this for many years and had been thrilled when she became pregnant once married, secretly believing this new baby would "cure" her guilt. The six-week contract we arranged together gave her the space to consider whether she wanted to tell her husband about her termination and to grieve the loss of the first baby. She asked to see me for one session about a year later, and she brought her two-month-old baby boy to see me.

Infertility problems

A GP may refer a woman or a couple for counselling who are experiencing difficulty in conceiving. As with the above, there may be issues surrounding an earlier termination that need to be worked through in counselling, or the doctor may suspect there are other emotional, rather than medical, reasons why the couple cannot conceive. The counsellor is in a better position in a six-week, unhurried assessment to uncover what these emotional blocks might be. Feeling held and understood, the couple may go on to conceive quite quickly, and the six sessions can be spread out over several months for support, or they may wish to come back once the child is born just to check that all is well in their emotional response to the child. The counsellor should never underestimate the emotional power of the holding environment of counselling in primary care.

With infertility problems, of course, there is always the scenario that ends in no child because of insurmountable physical problems, and in this case there will be grief, sometimes very complicated grief, to contend with. Women and men often grieve differently, and it is important that this is identified in order that the couple get appropriate help, either together or individually. In my experience, it is better if this can happen within the setting of primary care, even if the six-session contract has to be extended, as often the couple will be in a regressed state and will need the support of that "family" environment; the "family" environment, in this instance, being a family of professionals, such as counsellor, GP, consultant, or nurse, etc.

When a child or adolescent is presented as being problematic

A person may consult their GP about their child or adolescent who is displaying uncontrollable behaviour, school refusal, being bullied, withdrawn, truanting, etc. Parents can find this kind of behaviour very distressing and believe that the problem lies entirely with the child. Some GPs will know that this is not the case and have the wisdom to investigate the situation further with the parent or parental couple. With sensitive handling, a referral to the counsellor can help the parents look at the whole family situation and get an idea of family dynamics, which may be malfunctioning to a greater or lesser degree. The "problem" may well be seated in the parents or parent regressing and/or over-identifying with the developmental conflicts of the child or adolescent's life process. People do not normally identify or understand how their own childhood difficulties can be resurrected by experiencing their child's life problems. Old emotional wounds may be opened but, with careful handling, the counsellor may encourage a parent or parents to receive help for them or agree to family therapy.

Example: Angela

Angela's GP asked me to see her nine-year-old daughter. This was at a time when GP's could refer children to an in-house primary care counsellor. I suggested I contact the mother and ask her to come in to see me for a session on her own so that she could share with me her worries concerning her daughter's behaviour. Angela had been separated from her husband for several years, but had cordial relations with him over the daughter, even though the husband had remarried. The father had recently died in tragic circumstances, and the daughter was displaying what turned out to be an unusual grief reaction: sleep walking and aggressive behaviour. I had just two sessions with Angela. What soon became obvious to me was that, because she was the ex-wife, she had not been invited to the funeral and nor was anyone expecting her to grieve. Angela was finding her daughter's grief difficult to bear because no one was hearing her own grief. I heard her grief and met her need to express it, and her daughter ceased her troublesome behaviour and nocturnal wanderings.

Not all childhood problem behaviour can be dealt with so easily, and each case must be taken on its merits.

Personality disorder

We looked earlier at how this may manifest in the counselling room and how one might recognize signs of this disabling condition. A person may present for counselling who has a personality that causes him/herself, other people, and the person's family problems in everyday life. It must not be forgotten that they are also prey to the same losses, reactive depressions, and anxiety as anyone else. People with these problems have sometimes alienated staff at the surgery by perhaps displaying very dependent or aggressive behaviour in the past. Consequently, they may have a "reputation" that goes before them into the counselling room.

This "difficult" patient can create strong reactions in the primary care staff who care for and treat them. Those professional reactions, in turn, may cause more difficulties for the patient. The staff may retreat from the patient emotionally and from their painful personal experience. The "difficult patient" is not a label that one will find as a *DSM* category. It is more that the patient evokes feelings that are difficult for the counsellor or doctor when they are in that person's presence. Hinshelwood phrases this as, "finding our humanitarian interest stymied" (Hinshelwood, 1999). We may feel intruded upon and manipulated as they appear to directly and deliberately (although unconsciously) interfere with our feelings. We can feel impelled to conform to a pattern imposed by the patient, so that we begin to feel provoked and we can end up behaving just as the patients needs us to, that is, rejecting and hostile (Pines, 1978). The experience is disagreeable and the situation can feel as though the patient is abusing our help, our time, and us. The patient who does not complement our helping stance confounds us; they appear to refuse to receive our help and a negative and un-negotiable wrangle can ensue.

That is not all. In a setting like the GP surgery or mental health department of a hospital, this "wrangle" can be acted out within the professional caring team in a way that is unhelpful, unless the unconscious dynamics can be unravelled. It can be very difficult to keep in the forefront of your mind that the person in front of you is suffering from unspeakable pain; unspeakable, because the origins of that pain are almost certainly preverbal and, as such, can only be projected into the psyche of the counsellor to be dealt with. In psychodynamic terms, this is called projective identification.

The person may have multiple psychopathologies, as was the case with a man referred to a trainee in placement that I had the privilege to supervise.

Example: John

John was well known to the staff of the surgery, as he suffered from obsessive–compulsive disorder, had high dependency needs due to the complication of being agoraphobic, suffering from hypochondria, and an intense fear of illness in those close to him. The lead counsellor in the practice carried out the assessment and decided that as he was now presenting what seemed like normal grief, she referred him to the trainee to talk about the loss of his mother and his emotions of grief. This turned out to be a very difficult contract for the counsellor and patient to fulfil, and salutary lessons were learnt all round. However, although it was an inappropriate referral for a psychodynamic trainee, this case is a good example of how difficult patient psychopathology can disrupt the dynamics in a primary care team so much that the staff can act out that pathology. I believe the lead counsellor referred the patient to the trainee in good faith, not realizing she was unconsciously denying the truth of the matter, that is, that this person could never experience, or work through, normal grief in an uncomplicated way. The lead counsellor (mentor) "knew" this patient, and that he had been passed around the primary care staff for many years, as if too hot to handle.

People with these kinds of problems in the community have the misfortune to be emotionally disabled and, although often difficult, need and deserve societal support.

The advice seeker

When a patient comes into counselling asking for advice, it is important during the assessment session to assess whether that is all that the patient is asking for. Asking for advice may be the habitual way that this person makes contact with others and thus he/she will require help to uncover underlying emotional need. He/she may be asking the counsellor to help with coping strategies and may be displaying a high need for control of emotions and situations. A six-week CBT contract is often a good choice in the first instance. This length of CBT contract on the basis of immediate need, offered at times of change and transition, can help a person who displays poor coping strategies and social skills or inability to control aggression or sexual impulses appropriately. The six weeks can be usefully employed in doing some work on their behaviour or learning coping strategies.

However, the six weeks could be used to pave the way for a referral for longer-term CBT or psychodynamic counselling with either a private practitioner or within a charitable counselling agency that tailors their fee to the client's ability to pay.

When the GP has been the "counsellor"

A patient who has been consulting with the same doctor for 30–40 years for all matters, be they physical or emotional, may feel rejected and let down by their GP when he/she refers them to a counsellor. The person may feel the doctor has lost patience with them and their problems. The GP may be making the referral from the right motives, but has not been sufficiently sensitive to how this might make the patient feel. The patient may feel resentful, angry, and can quickly give the counsellor the impression that they are second best. It has been my experience that this issue needs to be sensitively addressed as soon as possible, and without loss of face for the patient. Some time will need to be spent empathizing with how this has left the person feeling before the issue that the GP thought needed attention in counselling can be approached. This situation can lead to no contract being agreed, as what the patient really wants is regular contact with his/her GP for reassurance and security, not an in-depth exploration of his/her life or psyche. However, depending upon how sensitively the counsellor deals with this situation, the patient, at a later date, may decide to come back to see the counsellor when it is his/her own idea. Then, an appropriate six-week contract can be negotiated with a clear and manageable focus or goal, perhaps looking at why the person has the need to consult with his/her GP for reassurance about their health.

If the patient does return voluntarily at a later date, a cognitive approach can help him/her to address health anxiety by gently challenging the person's view of him/herself and to reframe their experience of illness, diagnosis, and treatment in more constructive ways.

Example: Harry

Harry had been consulting his doctor all his married life with normal health issues, for example, hypertension, an ulcer, and a bad back. The GP has noticed over the years that when Harry consults him over any health issue, the conversation always ends up about his relationship with his stepdaughter, and the frictions this causes between him and his wife. The surgery has just taken on a counsellor, so the doctor thinks Harry could be helped by a rather more in-depth talk about the issues involved. What the GP may not take into consideration is the trust that has been built up for Harry between them and also just how helpful those "chats" have been for

Harry over the years. The GP may be able to see how Harry could be helped to move on in his relationship with both his stepdaughter and his wife, but has missed the fact that Harry is not actually asking for that to happen.

Loss, grief reactions, and mourning

Grief is a reaction to loss and can manifest psychologically and physically. Mourning is the psychological processing of grief reactions, as the person moves towards being able to let go of what or who has been lost. Unacknowledged and unresolved grief can lurk behind many of the symptoms and problems that are presented in the GP surgery. When asked why they are feeling depressed, a person may have no idea, but after careful and sensitive questioning, some kind of loss in the past is revealed. Unexplained physical symptoms can also often be covering a significant loss and the need to grieve.

Uncomplicated grief

By an uncomplicated grief, I mean a situation where the patient has suffered the death of a loved one and to which they are having an appropriate reaction. A six-week contract with the counsellor at the right time can help a patient feel supported and understood when they themselves feel they cannot "burden" family and friends any longer. The most appropriate time for this counselling will often be gauged by the patient, and is not necessarily straight after the loss has occurred. Anniversaries, such as birthdays or the first Christmas, can be especially hard, and family and friends may not be sufficiently sensitive to realize this, or, as I have already indicated, the person may feel a burden to others at this time, or they may be a very private person. This patient may begin by apologizing for "wasting" the counsellor's time, but are usually reassured that they are not. They may wish to share photographs with the counsellor as an unspoken recognition of how important the dead person still is to them. Some patients may wish to share happy memories, or, in the event of the relationship being poor between the patient and the deceased, they may need to express negative emotions without being judged or misunderstood.

Complicated grief

This can occur when the death has not been straightforward and by natural causes. Think for a moment how differently a person may feel if the person committed suicide or was murdered. Another scenario is when a loved one has died in a different country and alone, or has died in a horrific road accident. When there has been some poor practice or negligence after a medical procedure in hospital, the person may find it difficult to move on from anger with the medical profession.

A complicated grief reaction may be suitable for a six-week counselling contract and this should be decided in the assessment session. The counsellor must be on the lookout for other complicated grief reactions the person may have suffered in the past and how far the person has integrated these issues and recovered from them.

The person may be suffering from post traumatic stress disorder from cumulative loss and trauma. It is unlikely that a six-week contract could address the underlying issues in this situation, in which case an extended, six-week assessment could help the person towards the longer-term help that they may need.

Pathological grief reaction

The most obvious sign of pathological grief reaction is where the patient is stuck in one of the phases of the grief process. I do not mean to imply that the process of grief will normally follow neatly through a pattern: numbness followed by depression, followed by anger, etc., but a GP may refer someone for counselling who does not appear to be recovering normally from a death or other significant loss. As with the above, it is important in the assessment to look at how this person has dealt with loss in the past and what might be different about this particular loss. Their unique reaction might be to be continually angry, depressed, or yearning for the lost person, which has the effect of them not being able to take up life and begin living again. The counsellor discovers the problem to be, for instance, that the person remains stuck in grief through a feeling of overwhelming guilt at wanting to begin to enjoy life again and move forward. Another example is when a person is receiving some secondary gain in remaining stuck, such as more attention from other loved ones. Often, once the counsellor has gently pointed out what may be happening, this can unlock the person's process enough for them to move forward. However, for some people, being the "victim" of life's losses has become a way of life. If this is the case, it is unlikely that a six-week contract will move the person on to normal functioning.

A person presenting with a physical symptom similar to that from which the dead person died can also be a way of pathologically "holding on to" the dead person and somehow keeping them alive and not separated from the patient.

Terminal and life-limiting illness

It is important for the counsellor to ask him/herself some searching questions about how counselling someone with a terminal or life-limiting illness would be difficult for them. Death and disability are not well integrated into everyday life in our society and we have an investment in denying their existence. If the counsellor's caseload is unbalanced, with several patients in this category, he/she may experience compassion fatigue or suffer secondary trauma. By this, I mean the counsellor suffering vicarious trauma as a result of being bathed in hearing too much horrific pain and suffering. Personally, I have found counselling someone with multiple sclerosis the most difficult. I was not prepared for the guilt I would feel for being healthy and able to live life to the full. I was unprepared for the fact that the person was normal in every way except for their illness and that they had no more additional strength than any other person to deal with the issues surrounding their illness.

People with terminal and life-limiting illness still have all the other vicissitudes of life to deal with, and often feel rejected and enraged. In other words, as the counsellor, you will often find yourself in the presence of someone who is just like you in all human ways but who is also facing unspeakable loss.

The contract in these cases may consist of giving the person "permission" to feel what they feel and to give them the opportunity to take some time out from being the "sick" one in the family.

Most people who are dying or have a life-limiting illness need and want to live as fully as they can each day; they do not stop having the same desires and aspirations, hurts and anger as the rest of us. The counsellor must never underestimate how cathartic the ventilation of strong emotions can be in a holding and containing environment.

Breakdown of relationship between patient and GP

Sometimes, the covert problem being presented to the counsellor is a patient's breakdown of their relationship with the GP. This problem may well be dressed up as something else, and sensitivity is needed to tease out the real distress, as there may be a danger of collusion between counsellor and patient (or counsellor and GP). Underlying this problem may be issues to do with authority and some unrealistic expectations. A six-week contract can be used to separate the issues with the person and help them reach a healthier attitude towards themselves. For example, helping a person to see how the GP has come to represent an authority figure from the patient's past can be a revelation to them, something that they have never given thought to before. If they are able to take on board that the GP is not going to judge them or try to make them feel disempowered, they may gain a healthier attitude towards what the GP can offer.

When the patient brings another person into the room with them

This situation is not as unusual as it might seem in the primary care setting. A young mother may arrive bringing her baby or young child, or a young lady may bring her mother or her boyfriend. A husband may come in with his wife. By accepting this situation in the first instance, it is possible to reduce the need for either you or the patient to become defensive. In fact, it is prudent for the counsellor to normally take the stance of "accepting what is", as this is usually the best way to begin to move forward. Empathic thinking about why the person may need someone else with them can help you to make a suitable response and to deal with the situation in a helpful way. Remember that if a person is accompanied, it is often the need of the accompanying person that is being met, and the counsellor will need to address this with sensitivity.

Example: Joan and Cliff

Joan was referred for counselling by her GP with anxiety and depression. Her husband, Cliff, came into the counselling room with her for her first session. Cliff began by saying that he was not at all sure that counselling was what his wife needed and asking what would I be doing with her. He was obviously well educated and articulate, and a concerned husband. He told me that his wife had become depressed since he retired from business, and they could afford to go privately if necessary. What I picked up and voiced was that he had concerns about whether I would be an experienced enough counsellor to help his wife. He seemed pleasantly surprised that I had not become defensive about his concerns and that I was happy for him to stay while I conducted my assessment. After about ten minutes, he said he was happy to leave his wife in my hands.

Social needs

In any primary care practice some patients will present for counselling with mainly social needs; that is, they need help with housing, benefits, and home care, etc. As mentioned earlier, a person's GP becomes the first port of call when there is need, and a referral to a counsellor is not uncommon, as the doctor may feel that the counsellor has more time to assess the person's ability to obtain appropriate help from Social Services. In many people's minds, Social Services and the NHS are the same thing, and they find it difficult to take on board that they are separate and need to be accessed accordingly. Many consider that it is "they" out there that should be meeting their needs. Authority figures are lumped together into a kind of universal "parent", of which the GP is the most accessible. What is useful in a situation like this is a six-week contract that is mainly about patiently and empathically educating and facilitating the person to seek out the help they need elsewhere. For some, the Citizens Advice Bureau can be a very helpful next port of call. However, in some instances, this can be a very sad exercise for the counsellor, as he/she must stand by watching a person who does not have sufficient strength or mature strategies to cope with their life in today's society. These patients may return for counselling many times during their life cycle, until they are eventually housed in a residential or nursing home.

Additional issues

Non-attendance

Because of financial constraints in primary care, it is necessary for the patient to forfeit his/her session through non-attendance. Of course, there would be exceptions to this rule when the non-attendance is due to genuine illness or accident. It is a sad fact that not everyone is able to make use of the counselling that is on offer in primary care. Immaturity or personality problems may mean that a person is incapable of making the necessary commitment.

Example: Joseph

Joseph was referred for counselling after he had consulted his GP about his obesity. He also had the related problems of type two diabetes and back pain. He had been prescribed medication for his diabetes and his back pain had been investigated and found to be muscular. The GP had also prescribed a course of graded exercise at the local gym. The assessment session went quite well, with Joseph showing some insight into his problems. He failed to attend the next session, and in the third had the attitude that he had been sent to the gym and counselling and that he was being punished. Although during the session the counsellor investigated this feeling with him, and Joseph seemed to have made a link with punishments in his earlier life, his wife telephoned before the next session to say he was too ill to attend counselling any more.

Special cases

From time to time, the counsellor will need to make a case with the patient's GP for longer-term counselling to be carried out within the primary care setting because of a genuine inability to access it elsewhere. It has been my experience that most GPs are happy to sanction this. They can see that not to do so would cause undue distress and hardship and/or many more NHS resources would have to be utilized if the counselling cannot happen within the primary care setting.

Example: Emily

Emily was deemed unfit to look after her children, who, over the years, have each been fostered and put up for adoption. Now, with a new partner, she had given birth to another child who was made a ward of court. Her new partner was named as the primary carer for the child, and counselling for the mother was made mandatory for Emily with a view to the new baby being allowed to stay permanently with the couple. This would happen only if counselling were deemed to have helped the mother to parent the child more adequately. Obviously, in this instance, many issues arose for Emily, not the least of which was anger towards Social Services and her reaction to her multiple loss. The main focus of the counselling was Emily's own mother's inability to sufficiently mother her. In this case, there was a good outcome, with Emily and her new partner being allowed to keep the new baby after eighteen months of counselling.

Consistent lateness

It is very difficult to carry out a successful six-week contract with someone who consistently arrives late for his/her sessions. It is sometimes possible to get across to the patient that it is they who are missing out on valuable time for themselves, but often any reference that the counsellor makes about time-keeping is experienced as punitive, which, over the short term, is virtually impossible to do work with therapeutically.

Late disclosures of information

Late disclosures (after the second or third week of the contract) of relevant information, such as abuse in childhood or present harmful behaviour, often make effective short-term counselling untenable. Brain biology research suggests possible links between childhood psychological trauma and later physical pathology

(Teicher et al., 2003). When this is the case in the consulting room, it is unlikely to be disclosed in the assessment session and an on-going six-week assessment may be needed to facilitate the person to access longer-term therapy.

Other disclosures may be about not taking life-saving medication, or murderous intent. Once the disclosure has been made, a new contract will need to be negotiated with the GP and the patient in order to tackle the consequences of the new information.

Key issues

1. The trainee counsellor on placement should always work within their competency.
2. The counselling frame in the primary care setting is likely to suffer more impingements than in other settings.
3. The extent of the contract and the time-limited nature of counselling must be clearly imparted to the patient.
4. Different PCTs around the country give varying priority to counselling in primary care.
5. Loss comprises a large component of the work in primary care.

CHAPTER TWELVE

Approaches to different categories of patient and presenting problem

D ue to the nature of the setting, the counsellor in primary care will see patients who fall into many different categories; similarly, with the nature of the problems presented.

All the issues that are covered in Chapter Four may be presented by any one of the categories of patient examined below. The counsellor will need to adapt their approach to each.

In primary care, the counsellor is working at the "coalface", where the client base will be different from those seen in private or agency counselling and is often more challenging. Counselling in this setting is free at the point of need, and, therefore, money is not an issue. For most patients referred to the surgery counsellor, this will be their first experience of counselling, and because paying for counselling will not have entered their heads, only a relatively small proportion of surgery patients find the motivation to move on to longer-term private counselling, even when they agree with the counsellor that it would be the best course for them.

The counsellor must "cut the cloth" to fit the patient in this setting. It can seem like quite a hurdle for the counsellor to take on board that most of the patients they see will not reach their full potential as human beings. However, the counsellor may find a person's desire to motivate themselves to achieve what they can in very difficult circumstances very rewarding. The counsellor must also realize that they may see these people for a six-week contract, perhaps on a yearly basis, for the duration of their employment in the same primary care setting. Remember that it is all right to do what you can in small ways rather than try to save the world!

The patient suffering chronic pain: pain management

A patient with chronic pain not associated with terminal or life-threatening illness may be stuck in a vicious circle of pain, depression, and reduced mobility that seriously circumscribes their life. CBT and problem-management approaches can help to mobilize the person's psychological coping resources, thus enhancing the effects of medication and helping the person to come to terms with changes of lifestyle: that is, it can help the person adjust to their situation.

Example: George

George, a male nurse aged fifty, has had periods of severe back pain since a skiing accident. He is on long-term sick leave and spends long, painful days at home while his wife works in a high-powered job and has long working days. He has put on weight, and his inactivity has tipped him into feeling depressed. He has not suffered with depression in the past, but now feels unmotivated to help himself, even to have the pain properly investigated. A CBT approach could validate and support him, while offering a formulation, motivation, and strategies to address his depression, weight gain, and passive reaction to what is happening to him.

The "ripe" patient

A "ripe" patient is someone who is exactly ready for counselling. They are often intelligent, if not well educated, insightful, and at a place in their life where they want to make changes and gain a deeper understanding of how they relate to others and to themselves.

These people are often a counsellor's favourite type of person to counsel. Their main needs are for affirmation of thoughts and ideas, and validation of feelings. They will have good ego strength, although they may have low self-esteem and little confidence in their abilities. Consequently, they may not value themselves or their abilities and will often have been undervalued by others. They can demonstrate a good ability to love, work, and play, and they generally have good family relationships. They make good use of a six-week CBT or psychodynamic contract, as they are ready to make use of validation and encouragement to enter an investigative partnership with the counsellor.

Example: Dora

Dora had been sexually abused as a teenager and was poorly educated, which left her feeling inferior. Two of her children had special educational needs and, she believed, were not being given the help they required. She was able, with encouragement and affirmation, to fight for her children's education in a way that had not been done for her when she was a child. She was able to acquire the help for her children, and the discovery that she had the skills to achieve gave her the satisfaction and the boost that she needed to carry on with her quite difficult life.

The very young patient

Most GP surgery counsellors would not see children or young people under the age of eighteen. However, this may change with the new government guidelines. Also, many young people over the age of eighteen in our cultural climate are still quite emotionally immature, and this must be borne in mind when counselling them. We must remember that young people today have often grown up in a very protected environment, due to parents perceiving danger around every corner. Also, health and safety regulations have given the message to society that accidents are totally preventable. This prevailing societal attitude may hinder our young people from making the mistakes and taking the risks necessary for growing independence and maturity.

As these young people are often just beginning to separate emotionally from their parents, a look at core beliefs, central conflicts, aims, and goals can be very helpful to them. It can give them the life tools to develop a focused approach to life, at the same time as valuing and validating their feelings. Young people often have fears surrounding what is "normal", and some time spent looking at what is normal for them can go a long way to exploding the myth of normality. Sometimes, investigating with the young person just what happens in their life that may perpetuate feelings of low self-esteem, lack of confidence, and what makes them anxious is what is needed. These are the kind of issues that may get addressed in a nurturing home environment, but often people grow up in environments that are not conducive to healthy emotional growth.

These young patients often respond well to an eclectic approach, the counsellor using tools and skills from both CBT and psychodynamic models.

Example: Simon (aged twenty-one)

Simon had been educated to "A" level at a private school. As the school was out in the countryside and could not be accessed by bus, he had been taken and collected from school each day by his mother, with whom he had a close relationship. His father had left the marital home when he was quite small, but Simon still had regular contact with him. Simon was a quiet boy who achieved very well at school. However, he had no idea what he wanted to study at university, but knew that he was expected to go, with which he complied. His father wanted him to study law or medicine. When he was referred for counselling, he had failed to settle into two universities after attempting the subjects that his father had chosen for him. He told the counsellor he had had a "breakdown" at both universities, and was now living back at home with his mother. Simon had not enjoyed studying the subjects and had found fending for himself and getting around the universities' towns very challenging, as he had never used a map or bus before. He said his mother loved having him at home, as she was lonely.

By using an eclectic approach, looking at both Simon's core beliefs about himself, his parents, and the world around him, and giving him the opportunity to express some of his overwhelming anger and feelings of insecurity and uncertainty about his future, the primary care counsellor was able to help Simon to look at what he wanted for himself in the future and how he might find the motivation to achieve it.

The elderly patient

It is important that the elderly section of society is not written off as "just old", as some useful short-term counselling work can be accomplished with all age groups. Depression is common in the elderly and can be helped with counselling, with or without accompanying medication. A sensitive and respectful approach is needed, as the person will almost certainly have had more life experience than the counsellor, and this needs to be acknowledged and used to help them find solutions to new problems. Solution-focused counselling and/or a CBT approach can often be very helpful in this situation, as long as time is also allowed for the ventilation of strong emotion, perhaps about growing old and having to make the transition to being less mobile. The person may have already lost several of their family members, or may be the last remaining out of a group of friends. Remember that a person's self-respect and dignity at this late age can make the difference between a tolerable and an intolerable existence.

The phobic patient

Many people suffer from phobias that are life-limiting and cause a great deal of distress. Depending upon the form the phobia takes, some patients respond well to a short-term CBT approach, but, in most cases of phobic reaction, longer-term CBT or psychodynamic counselling is more helpful by gradually uncovering the meaning behind the phobic feelings and behaviour. This kind of longer-term help is not usually available in the primary care setting.

One of the most helpful things for the patient is that the counsellor takes the problem seriously and acknowledges how disabling phobias can be. We can all identify with an irrational fear of spiders, but a phobia of flying or staircases is, for some, less understandable, and it may well have been the person's experience that their fears are dismissed as trivial. There are longer-term, in-depth CBT and psychodynamic methods of helping someone with a phobia, which look at underlying issues.

Culture and difference

Culture

Apart from the obvious cultural differences of colour, race, and religion, there are the less obvious differences. Each family and section of the community has its own culture. For instance, the criminal culture has very different values to those considered to be the norm for our society. In a criminal culture, it is getting caught that is frowned upon and justice is about looking after your own kind. The frame of reference in this instance is not what is right or wrong, but what is shameful or honourable in that particular culture.

It likely that in the counsellor's career in primary care, he/she will have dealings with the travelling community, who may have quite different beliefs and values to their own. It may be difficult for the counsellor to offer unconditional acceptance. It is in situations like these that one's prejudices surface, and if we are to help the person to make a difference to their life we need to challenge those prejudices.

The physically disabled patient

It is easy, inadvertently, to take a prejudiced and patronizing stance towards a patient who is physically disabled. This is not helpful to the person in question. It is essential that, when making contact to arrange the first meeting, the counsellor discuss with the patient any special needs they may have regarding the logistics of the building. A different room arrangement may need to be set up in order for the person to access counselling.

The patient with a learning difficulty

Although counselling someone who has a learning difficulty is often seen as a specialist area, there are very few specialists. The two main things to remember are that these people have the same emotional life as anybody else and are subject to the same adaptations of personality: for example, they may be emotionally stable or labile, and they may be very talkative or very quiet. Second, because their learning difficulty often affects every area of their lives, they may find it difficult to transfer what is learnt in one situation into another. Counselling can work well if the counsellor is prepared to give the extra listening, understanding, and patience that is needed.

Example: Paul

Paul was allocated to a trainee on placement in a GP surgery. The trainee was somewhat taken aback, as she had not been told of Paul's learning difficulty. Paul was in his early forties and lived with his eighty-one-year-old mother. Reading between the lines, it seemed probable that Paul's mother also had a learning difficulty, as it transpired that nothing had been put in place for Paul to maximize his potential or have any kind of separate life.

Paul had become depressed and somehow found his way to the GP. It transpired that Paul's mother was beginning to deteriorate physically and mentally, and Paul could not cope with her. He was able to do the shopping, but his mother had stopped cooking or doing the washing and needed help with personal care. The counsellor listened very carefully to how Paul was feeling and was sensitive in affirming what he could do, and was able to investigate with him those areas in which he felt he needed help at home. She was amazed at how competent Paul could be in accessing help from Social Services once he had the "permission" and encouragement to do so.

By the end of his contract, which the GP agreed could be extended by six extra sessions, he was beginning to go out on his own for his own pleasure. He told the counsellor he had always wanted to join the library, and she was able to encourage him to speak to the librarian about how to join and for help with choosing books that he could read. It was a privilege for me to supervise this piece of work. At the end, we began to wonder whether, given the help when he was younger, this man might have been able to achieve much greater things.

The counsellor would have liked to carry on counselling him in an ongoing contract but, as so often happens in this line of work, she had to let him go to make his own way. She found this difficult, but letting go is a lesson we all have to learn.

The terminally or chronically ill patient

In the face of such overwhelming pain and distress it can be very difficult for a counsellor to see a way to make a difference with the patient. However, the counsellor may be amazed at people's courage and perseverance and how a six-week counselling contract can be used to help a person come to terms with what cannot be changed. With careful investigation there are almost always things that can be changed, and it is a privilege to help in facilitating this. The patient may have become accustomed to being "at the mercy" of others and have temporarily forgotten that they can still be proactive in their lives.

The patient who has suffered childhood trauma

People who have suffered childhood trauma are often left permanently emotionally and developmentally disabled. The trauma or abuse that the person suffered as a child may have been physical, sexual, mental, and/or emotional. This disability leaves the person with permanent special needs.

It can be argued that each one of us has our own special needs, and when we seek out counselling for ourselves, it is those needs that we take with us. However, there is a section of our community who, because of life's many disasters, are left permanently damaged and who will always need help to cope with life as we live it today.

The aggressive patient

Unfortunately, some patients become verbally aggressive when they feel the counsellor is not giving them what they want. There are many reasons for this, and often the material gathered in the assessment session gives clues as to which reason relates to this patient. The counsellor must always bear in mind that he/she, too, may feel an aggressive or angry response to a patient, and being aware of this from the start will make it less likely that he/she will act it out in a session.

Possible reasons for an aggressive response

The patient may:

- feel "sent" for counselling;
- have expectations of counselling which cannot objectively and/or realistically be met within the six-week time scale;
- have an impulsive, aggressive, or paranoid personality, which may or may not come into the category of a disorder;
- find that their transference to the counsellor makes it difficult for them to respond in any other way, due to unresolved and unacknowledged issues from the past;
- unconsciously be aware that they have been made a scapegoat or identified as the patient by their dysfunctional family;
- find that their normal frustrations with the imperfect world of the NHS system gets the better of them, as it can for all of us.

Understanding why a person may be reacting in an aggressive way and avoiding making a defensive responsive can help to forestall an abortive counselling contract. These things can be overcome with an imaginative and sensitive approach.

The silent patient

As with the above, the counsellor is likely to glean sufficient clues during the assessment session as to why the patient finds it difficult to communicate. It may simply be that in their normal life no one listens to what they have to say or takes them seriously. It is unlikely that they will be silent in the assessment, as you may well be asking them specific questions. But they may go on to expect you to ask questions in subsequent sessions, and find it very difficult that you do not. Once this expectation is addressed and silences are thought about carefully together, the problem may be successfully ameliorated. I say may be, as it may not necessarily be the case, and other techniques may need to be employed. The counsellor may find him/herself working very hard in the sessions, and this alone can give clues to what may be going on in the patient's inner world. This can be tentatively looked at and/or challenged with the person, using Socratic questioning.

The patient suffering from a mental illness

Sometimes a patient who is suffering from a mental illness, such as schizophrenia, but who is being adequately treated with medication, may need counselling for a specific event, such as depression, close bereavement, or other sudden life-changing or life-limiting event or transition.

The patient presenting sexual dysfunction

As mentioned above, information gained during the assessment session will often inform the counsellor whether the type of sexual issue being presented is suitable for short-term counselling within the primary care setting. If the issue is deemed not to be suitable for what the counsellor can provide, then some investigations into what is available outside the setting will be necessary. Depending upon the patient's ability to seek that help, the counsellor may set up a six-week contract in order to allow the patient to ventilate feelings about the situation and to facilitate the patient making their own enquiries, either from their GP or from another agency. Relate have counsellors specifically trained to help with sexual dysfunction.

A patient with issues around gender and sexual orientation

Homosexuality, trans-sexualism, transvestism, having sexual addiction, or unique sexual predilections are very distressing for some individuals, and a six-week contract can help a person unravel their thoughts and feelings in order to see their way forward in life.

The patient suffering from an eating disorder and other self-harming behaviour

Self-harming behaviour is often a secret activity, and so a person may present a different problem to their GP. It is not until the person comes for counselling that this behaviour may be disclosed. For many, it may be a cry for help when it first occurs, and this is frequently in adolescence. However, it is more usual that by the time the patient arrives to see the counsellor, the problem behaviour is entrenched and the origins less obvious than when the person is younger. Short-term psychodynamic or CBT counselling is unlikely to help with longer-term outcomes, but can provide a basis for hope provided the person is sufficiently motivated to help themselves. However, even with great motivation on the part of both counsellor and patient in a long-term contract, management of the problem is often the best that can be achieved.

The eating and self-harm disorders displayed by a patient affect the whole family and are often an indicator of distress or dysfunction within that family. A referral for family therapy can be useful.

The patient suffering from chronic fatigue syndrome/ myalgic encephalitis (ME)

The National Institute for Health and Clinical Excellence (NICE) guidance on the diagnosis and management of the above disabling condition emphasizes the need to negotiate management programmes with patients. The guideline recommends that cognitive behaviour therapy and graded exercise therapy should be available in secondary care, since they show "the clearest research evidence of benefit" (Baker & Shaw, 2007).

When a GP diagnoses CFS/ME and sets proceedings in motion for the patient to enter secondary NHS care, it can be helpful for the person waiting for their first consultation with a neurologist to see the counsellor in the primary care setting. It has been my experience that either CBT or supportive counselling is useful at this time to help the patient over the initial impact of the diagnosis. They will almost certainly have been battling with the symptoms for some time before consulting the doctor, and will have undergone a series of tests to rule out any other disease. At this initial stage, the counsellor can help with containing the anxiety surrounding what the patient feels may be a poor prognosis: in some cases, years of rest, pain, and lack of employment. Often, the person does not have the energy to engage in their usual leisure and hobbies, interests, or family activities, and this is a great loss for them. The GP will give advice on management and the counsellor can help with emotional support and help to facilitate changes in the patient's lifestyle and/or thinking about themselves in the light of the huge changes in their life.

The patient presenting addiction to alcohol, drugs, or tobacco

Some people are more prone to addiction than others and, when it is difficult for a GP to assess whether the addiction is physical or psychological, he/she may suggest counselling to try to unravel the underlying causes. A six-week contract with a primary care counsellor will not be a cure for addiction, and other measures will need to be discussed with the patient and support given to implement them.

Post traumatic stress disorder (PTSD)

It must be remembered that this disorder does not only occur after a major trauma in adult life, such as a car accident, terrorist bombing, mugging, etc., but can occur after prolonged physical, mental, or emotional abuse. Post traumatic stress in war combat veterans can take months or even years (in some cases, thirty years) to manifest after the event. For any of the above causes, the assessment plus six sessions could be used as an extended assessment before referring on.

When the person first presents for counselling, it may be the case that neither the GP nor the person have picked up that they have the disordered thoughts and symptoms associated with trauma. Any of the following symptoms could indicate possible PTSD:

- repetitive, intrusive thoughts, images, memories, dreams with accompanying distress;
- flashbacks with accompanying affect of fear;
- avoidance of places, activities, talking about the trauma;
- emotional numbness and distance from others;
- inability to think about the future and make normal plans;
- disturbed sleep patterns;
- irritability and outbursts of anger;

- difficulty in concentrating;
- permanently vigilant and easily startled;
- panic attacks.

Referring the patient on for longer-term therapy will almost certainly be necessary, as treatments for this condition do not fit into a rationed primary care service. However, one of the radical implications of the NICE (National Institute for Clinical Excellence) guidelines is that the focus for treatment services for PTSD should shift to primary care. Changes will need to be made in the delivery of primary care counselling for this disabling disorder. Turner (2007) points out the guidelines also emphasize that basic treatments last between eight and twelve sessions, that some sessions should be ninety minutes long, and that some people will require longer treatment. It has been my experience that a patient showing symptoms of PTSD can be helped with either longer-term psychodynamic or CBT counselling.

The treatments that NICE identifies for PTSD are trauma-focused cognitive–behavioural therapy (TF-CBT) and eye movement desensitization and reprocessing (EMDR). They identified that these treatments would, for most people, be better than drug treatments. Turner (*ibid.*) tells us of some new developments drawn from basic science in our understanding of the mental processes involved in PTSD. He speaks of current interest in the amygdala, a basic structure deep in the brain, which seems to be important as a means of alerting to danger. It appears to store emotionally charged memories of previous dangerous experiences. The amygdala automatically recognizes these patterns when the person finds himself or herself in a similar situation again. It responds much faster than the conscious thinking brain, and this organ allows us to react before we think. This gives us the advantage of escaping from danger, but it may malfunction and incorrectly trigger this alert/ fear response. When this happens in PTSD, recollections of a trauma intrude and the experience appears to be happening again as if in the present (flashbacks).

Further reading

A useful source for further information on post traumatic stress disorder is Brewin (2003).

Patients at risk

A patient is deemed to be at risk when his/her physical or mental life is being seriously endangered. Where violence in the family has been the norm for the person, he/she may not recognize the danger they are in or that anything can be done about it. The counsellor of this type of client may need to help him/her to mobilize outside help to minimize risk. This may seem more like social work, but, in some inner city and severely deprived areas of the country, this may make up a considerable amount of the requests from the primary care team.

Patient seriously deteriorated since the assessment session

A counsellor must use his/her integrity in this situation to assess whether other agencies need to be mobilized, for example, an immediate appointment with the GP or involvement by the crisis intervention team.

Example: Nora

Nora consulted with her GP a few days after her husband had suddenly abandoned her for a younger woman after twenty-eight years of marriage. They had no children and her family lived in a different country. The GP prescribed antidepressants, a short course of sleeping pills, and suggested she make an appointment to see the surgery counsellor. She did not take the antidepressants or make an appointment for counselling at that time. Instead, she decided to paint the outside of her house and landscape the garden to take her mind off her situation. This did not work for her, and she became very distressed and emotionally unstable. At this point, she made an appointment to see the surgery counsellor. She arrived in a state of physical disarray, wearing paint-splattered clothes, and unable to give a coherent account of her situation or how she felt.

The counsellor could see immediately that she could not function normally and was able to get her an urgent appointment with her GP, who suggested she go for assessment as an inpatient at the local psychiatric unit.

Vicarious traumatization

Vicarious traumatization (VT) is a situation that the counsellor of deeply traumatized patients can experience. Marion Crowley (2005) describes this process as psychic contamination, whereby the patient's emotional experience intrudes into our unconsciousness and that this occurs out of our awareness. Pearlman and Saakvitne (1995) suggest that as a consequence of our work with traumatized patients, we experience disruption to our beliefs and intrusive imagery. It is important to remember that VT is a common response and does not reflect the competence of the counsellor, but does alert them to their need for extra support from their supervisor and other professionals. In some severe instances, counsellors have had to stop working in this profession, as they may experience depression and troublesome somatic symptoms.

Key issues

1. Patients are individuals and should be seen as whole people,
2. Counsellors in primary care may at some time in their career suffer from compassion fatigue or vicarious traumatization. Monitoring one's own emotional well being is essential.

CHAPTER THIRTEEN

Waiting lists, endings, and referring on

As in all counselling, endings are very important, but in short-term counselling the ending is present all the time as part of the work and needs to be kept continually in sight in the counsellor–patient partnership.

When, how and where to refer a patient on

As with the above, referring on is a very important area that needs to be borne in mind by the counsellor throughout the work. For appropriate and successful referring on, the primary care counsellor must research what facilities there are in their working area and what might be appropriate for different types of client. Henderson (2007) points out that it is important that counsellors have a good grasp of which patients they are competent to see within the constraints of their service, and who they need to refer elsewhere. There are other types of help or support available for people who have emotional problems. Many voluntary organizations run support groups and self-help networks where a person can meet people who have similar experiences. It is helpful both to the counsellor and patient if he/she researches which of the above is available in their local area. There will be counselling agencies that offer a graded fee structure, some of whom will be able to offer counselling to people on state benefits. Many patients who need longer-term counselling or other types of support only need the counsellor to "walk beside them" while they do the research for themselves. In affluent parts of the country, many patients will be able to afford private counselling or psychotherapy, and it is useful if the primary care counsellor points them in the right direction by offering the details of several options. If a person has private health insurance, this widens the field of possible help.

Other therapies sometimes available on the NHS

Sometimes, it is necessary to refer the patient back to their GP in order for them to access other NHS therapies, such as cognitive analytic therapy, interpersonal psychotherapy, or systemic therapy. Humanistic and experiential psychotherapies, art therapy, music therapy, and drama therapy are also sometimes available. However, there is often a very long waiting list for these and they may also be rationed to a six-month duration.

Some people find physical therapies such as massage, acupuncture, yoga, and meditation, etc. helpful alongside counselling or instead of counselling. This is something the patient can discuss with the counsellor in order to discover what is most helpful for them and why. For example, someone who is stressed at work may find some form of relaxation activity most beneficial. Exercise is a proven way of helping mild to moderate depression, and sometimes all the person needs is "permission" to give him/herself what they need in the way of leisure pursuits or holidays. As mentioned before, the whole primary care environment, for some people, can carry a similar power to that of a parent over a child. This can work both to facilitate a patient towards a healthier outlook and lifestyle as well as fostering dependency. It is important that the primary care counsellor avoids colluding with the latter state of dependency unless it is obviously to the benefit of the patient.

Some patients latch on to the possibility of hypnotherapy being the panacea to all ills, because they have heard of impressive results.

Hypnotherapy can help with certain conditions, such as phobias and attempts to stop smoking. If the person is determined to try this type of treatment the surgery counsellor is in a good position to give advice on seeking hypnotherapy, or any other therapy, from a well-qualified practitioner, preferably a personal recommendation.

Waiting lists

Waiting lists are very important for managing the counselling service, and Waskett (2007) has given this considerable thought and attention in her article "How to cut the waiting list". This section looks carefully at what she has to say and adds additional ideas drawn from the author's experience.

Waiting lists have to be managed in order to minimize stress to counsellor and clients. Waskett (*ibid.*) has identified four key elements to consider, three of which are relevant to the remit of this book:

1.   Referrals.
2.   DNAs and cancellations.
3.   Enlisting patient motivation

Referrals

Waskett (*ibid.*) suggests that optimum, "bull's eye" referrals ensure that a waiting list will drop. By this, she means referrals that are appropriate, fit the service criteria, and involve patients who are interested in using the service.

Clear referral criteria

Having clear referral criteria accepted by the primary care team is not as easy as it sounds. However clear the counsellor is about referral criteria, a GP will often have their own agenda. It is important from the beginning that the counsellor gives clear guidelines about appropriate criteria for effective short-term counselling. The counsellor will need to spell out to, and possibly educate, the primary care team as to what constitutes an appropriate referral, and this is best achieved over time as the team begin to respect the counsellor's knowledge and experience.

Firm boundaries

Obviously, to comply with the above, firm boundaries have to be kept about who will receive counselling in the primary care setting. Again, this is not easy, as a patient's needs and distress can be overwhelming and can make quite an impact upon more than just the doctors. Nurses and reception staff may become involved and distressed in their turn, as a response to the patient.

In some instances, it may be necessary to say no to counselling for a particular patient. This can be very difficult for a new primary care counsellor who needs to become accepted by the staff, but, when it is necessary for this to happen, it is helpful to give a clear explanation to all concerned. Also, advice may be given on other suitable agencies that might be more appropriate for the person's needs, for example, Social Services, Citizens Advice Bureau, or an alcohol and addiction service.

Referral forms

It is very useful to develop a simple, brief, and clear referral form. This could be thought through with the GPs in the practice so that all are happy and clear about what is needed. A short explanation of the rationale behind the form and the nature of the service you provide may also be useful in cultivating cordial relationships with referrers. Updating referrers on any changes you make to the service is vital for good relations.

Contacting patients

Make sure there is provision on the referral form for a patient to give information about how they would like to be contacted, for example, by telephone, e-mail, or letter. It is much quicker to contact the patient by telephone, as the counsellor will know immediately whether the day and time being offered are suitable for them. It is important to get this right so as to avoid many DNAs (did not attend) and/or cancellations.

There also needs to be provision on the form for keeping any contact confidential from other members of the patient's family or other people living in the same home. Some patients prefer to be contacted at work in this instance.

DNAs and cancellations

If the counsellor can keep DNAs and cancellations to a minimum, it goes without saying that this will have a positive impact upon the effectiveness of counselling and the waiting list. This can be achieved by enabling the patient to attend in the first place. Telephone contact with the patient by the counsellor can allay his/her initial anxiety when they realize that they are dealing with an ordinary human being who is prepared to listen to and hear any difficulties they may have in attending. Problems may occur due to childcare arrangements, work times, or other reasons for only being able to attend at certain times of the day or week. Most people are used to having to attend their GP surgery to fit in with the surgery, and can be pleasantly surprised when a member of staff tries to accommodate their needs, if at all possible.

Obviously, DNAs and cancellations are directly linked to a patient's motivation for coming and also how well they feel they are tackling an agreed focus or goal. Patients are also helped to attend (or to decide that counselling is not for them) by being given clear guidelines and descriptions of what is expected of them and what they can expect from the counsellor. This can be put to them clearly and firmly in the assessment session.

If the waiting list is more than four weeks long, it is advisable to send a holding letter to the patient, informing them of how much longer they may expect to have to wait and also asking them to let the counsellor know if they still require counselling. Sometimes, a patient's problems may have been resolved by the time they receive their first appointment.

Enlisting patient motivation

Regarding patient motivation, Waskett says, "If we can engage the hope and motivation of clients they are much more likely to (a) come to appointments and (b) put energy into behaviours leading towards their therapeutic goals" (2007, p. 23).

Motivation can be a thorny issue, since many patients presenting for counselling in the primary care setting find themselves in the position of needing counselling because they lack motivation in their lives. This is not meant to sound derogatory, as motivation is a complex issue and the lack of it arises for many reasons, not least being social disadvantage and lack of timely encouragement in a person's life. Lack of self-esteem manifests itself in many ways and lack of motivation can be one of them. Thus, getting across to the patient that they are valued and worthy of help is an important aim for the counsellor as he/she makes contact with the patient. After all, it is the patient who is the expert upon him/herself, even if they are not aware of it, and a stance of respectful curiosity about the person's feelings, thinking, and behaviour goes a long way to gaining the person's trust and respect. Perhaps more important than conscious motivation is the very human desire to be in relationship with someone who cares and has time, and the hope of this can offer a magnetic impetus for attending regularly.

Key issues

1. In short-term counselling, the ending is ever present in the work.
2. Know when, how, and where to refer patients on in your area.
3. Put in place well organized waiting list and referral systems.

A short introduction to the neuroscience of psychotherapy

This section is for those who are interested in the study of what actually occurs in the brain when a person receives counselling or psychotherapy. This is but a short introduction to the subject, and at the end I recommend three books that I have found fascinating and informative, and which opens up a whole new way of thinking about the brain and the mind. It is not essential to know about these things to be effective as a therapist, but if you have an enquiring scientific mind, I can guarantee you will find one or all of these books absorbing.

It was Galen, a second-century Greek physician, who established the crucial role of the brain in controlling the body. Galen's work on brain function remained the state of the art right up to the twentieth century. He argued that the brain and its nerves are responsible for sensation, perception, emotion, planning, and action (Bainbridge, 2008).

Cozolino (2002), in the twenty-first century, says that the fundamental premise, put forth in his book, *The Neuroscience of Psychotherapy*, is that "any form of psychotherapy is successful to the degree to which it enhances positive experiential change and underlying neural network growth and integration" (p. 315). He puts forward that experience can build the neural structures of the brain and establish levels of the neurotransmitters that activate them. He believes that medication can help to establish neural network balance and integration that can then go on to enhance the benefits of psychotherapy.

In his Foreword to Cozolino's book, Siegel writes,

> As clinicians we immerse ourselves in the stories of individuals who come to us for help in feeling better and developing beyond old, maladaptive patterns of thought, behaviour, emotion, and relating. Over the years, the field of psychotherapy has developed numerous approaches that help people change. [p. ix]

Siegel sees as a puzzle, at present, just how the mind changes during the psychotherapeutic process, but believes that the new synthesis of neuroscience and psychotherapy seeks to help to solve this. What we do know is that these fundamental aspects of mind are greatly influenced by interpersonal relationships that connect people to each other within families and in psychotherapy.

Cozolino suggests that psychotherapy is an enriched environment tailored to encourage the growth and integration of neural networks regulating cognition, memory, emotion, and attachment. Neuroscience helps us to understand the process of how the brain is built and shaped by early interpersonal experiences, and how psychotherapy can create an interpersonal matrix capable of rebuilding it.

Cozolino sees that central to the interface of neuroscience and psychotherapy is the fact that human experience is mediated via two interacting processes. The first, he sees, is the expression of our evolutionary past via the organization and functioning of the nervous system; the second, the shaping of this neural architecture within the context of significant interpersonal relationships.

Having observed and worked with humans for the whole of my life so far, I agree with Cozolino when he states,

> The human brain is an "organ of adaptation" to the physical and social worlds; it is stimulated to grow and learn through positive and negative interactions. The quality and nature of our relationships are translated into codes within neural networks that serve as the infrastructure for both brain and mind. [Cozolino, 2002, p. 16]

He sees that it is through this translation of experience into neuro-biological structures that nature and nurture become one.

To counter this, Professor Steven Rose, having studied the human brain for forty-five years, in his interview with Gray (2007b), says he does not believe neuroscience will ever explain human psychology.

If the reader has enjoyed this taster of the liaison between neuro-science and psychotherapy, the works that I recommend are Gerhardt (2004), Cozolino (2002), and Rose (2006). Other helpful reading materials are BACP publications and information sheets.

REFERENCES

American Psychiatric Association (1994). *The Diagnostic and Statistical Manual of Mental Disorders (DSM-IV)*. New York: American Psychiatric Association.

Armstrong, K. (2007). *The Bible, The Biography* (p. 1). London: Atlantic Books.

Bainbridge, D. (2008). The sea horse and the cockerel's spur. *New Scientist, 197*: 40–43.

Baker, R., & Shaw, E. J. (2007). Diagnosis and management of chronic fatigue syndrome or myalgic encephalomyelitis (or encephalopathy): summary of NICE guidelines. *British Medical Journal, 335*: 446–448.

Beck, A. T., Rush, J., Shaw, B., & Emery, G. (1979). *Cognitive Therapy of Depression*. New York: Guilford Press.

Beck, A. T., Freeman, A., Davis, D. D., & Associates (1990). *Cognitive Therapy of Personality Disorders*. New York: Guilford Press.

Bion, W. (1961). *Experiences in Groups*. London: Tavistock.

Bion, W. (1962a). Learning from experience. In: *Seven Servants* (p. 89). New York: Jason Aronson, 1977.

Bion, W. (1962b). A theory of thinking. In: *Second Thoughts*. New York: Aronson, 1967.

Bion, W. (1970). *Attention and Interpretation*. In: *Seven Servants*. New York: Jason Aronson, 1977.

Bion, W. (2002). *Learning from Experience*. London: Karnac.

Bloom, B. L. (2001). Focused single-session psychotherapy: a review of the clinical and research literature. *Brief Treatment and Crisis Intervention*, 1: 75–86.

Bower, P. (2007). Confronting the hierarchy of evidence. *Healthcare Counselling and Psychotherapy Journal*, 7(4): 19.

Bond, T., & Sandhu, A. (2005). *Therapists in Court: Providing Evidence and Supporting Witnesses*. London: Sage.

Brewin, C. R. (2003). *Post-traumatic Stress Disorder: Malady or Myth?* New Haven, CT: Yale University Press.

Burnham, J. B. (1998). *Family Therapy*. London: Routledge.

Burton, M. (1998). *Psychotherapy, Counselling and Primary Mental Health Care*. Chichester: John Wiley.

Burton, M., & Henderson, P. (1997). *Counsellors' Experience of Supervision: Supervision* (Suppl. 3). Staines: Counselling in Primary Care Trust.

Butler, S. (2007). A way forward with PRN: the importance of two-way communication strategies that link research to practice and vice versa. *The Pychotherapist*, 36: 2.

Cambell, A. (1999). Single-session interventions: an example of clinical research in practice. *Australian and New Zealand Journal of Family Therapy*, 20: 183–194.

Cameron, C. L. (2007). Single session and walk-in psychotherapy: a descriptive account of the literature. *Counselling and Psychotherapy Research*, 7(4): 245–249.

Castillo, H. (2003). *Personality Disorder*. London: Jessica Kingsley.

Coe, J. (2008). Being clear about boundaries. *Healthcare Counselling and Psychotherapy Journal*, 8(1): 14.

Cozolino, L. J. (2002). *The Neuroscience of Psychotherapy: Building and Rebuilding the Human Brain*. New York: W. W. Norton.

Crowley, M. (2005). Vicarious traumatisation. *Counsellors & Psychotherapists in Primary Care Journal*, July.

Crowther, C. (2002). Supervising in institutions. In: J. Wiener, R. Mizen, & J. Duckham (Eds.), *Supervising and Being Supervised: A Practice in Search of a Theory* (pp. 100–117). London: Palgrave.

Curtis Jenkins, G. (1997). Setting the scene—supervision of counsellors in general practice—a four-fold model. In: *Supervision: Counselling in Primary Care Trust* (Suppl. 3). Staines: Counselling in Primary Care Trust.

Dalal, F. (2001). The social unconscious—a post Foulkesian perspective. *Group Analysis*, *34*(4): 539–555.

Department of Health (2001). *Treatment Choice in Psychological Therapies and Counselling: Evidence Based Clinical Guideline*. London: Department of Health.

Department of Health (2002). *Choosing Talking Therapies?* London: Department of Health.

Department of Health 2007(a). *Commissioning a Brighter Future: Improving Access to Psychological Therapies — Positive Practice Guide.* London: Department of Health [available at: www.dh.gov.uk/en/ Publicationsandstatistics/Publications/PublicationsPolicyAnd Guidance/DH_074556].

Department of Health (2007b). White Paper. *Trust, Assurance and Safety: The Regulation of Health Professionals* [available at: www.direct. gov.uk].

Dryden, W., & Feltham, C. (1992). Introduction to *Brief Counselling*. Milton Keynes: Open University Press.

East, P. (1995). *Counselling in Medical Settings*. Milton Keynes: Open University Press.

Ekstein, S., & Wallerstein, R. S. (1972). *The Teaching and Learning of Psychotherapy* (revised edn). London: Imago.

Elliot, R. (2002). Hermeneutic single case efficacy design. *Psychotherapy Research, 12*: 1–20.

Foulkes, S. H. (1990). Access to unconscious processes in the group–analytic group. In: *Selected Papers*. London: Karnac.

France, R., & Robson, M. (1997). *Cognitive Behavioural Therapy in Primary Care: A Practical Guide*. London: Jessica Kingsley.

Freeth, R. (2005). *Information Sheet P8: Psychopharmacology and Counselling and Psychotherapy*. Rugby: BACP.

Freeth, R. (2007). Working within the medical model. *Healthcare Counselling and Psychotherapy Journal, 7*(4): 7.

Freud, A. (1993). *The Ego and the Mechanisms of Defence*. London: Karnac.

Freud, S. (1923b). *The Ego and the Id. S.E., 19*: 3–66. London: Hogarth.

Freud, S. (1940a). *An Outline of Psycho-analysis. S.E., 23*: 141–207. London: Hogarth.

Fromm, E. (1977). *Psychoanalysis and Religion*. London: Yale University Press.

Gefter, A. (2008). Time's up. *New Scientist*, January: 26.

Gerhardt, S. (2004). *Why Love Matters: How Affection Shapes a Baby's Brain*. Hove: Brunner-Routledge.

Gilbert, P. (2000). *Counselling for Depression*. London: Sage.

Gray, P. (2007a). Biochemical imbalance in the brain—does it exist? *Therapy Today, 18*(8): 28–31.

Gray, P. (2007b). Making sense of neuroscience. *Therapy Today, 18*(8): 37–39.

Gray, P. (2007c). Care and protection for abused clients. *Therapy Today, 18*(7): 7–9.

Guggenbuhl-Craig, A. (1996). *Power in the Helping Profession.* Woodstock, CT: Spring.

Hawkins, P., & Shohet, R. (2000). *Supervising in the Helping Professions.* Milton Keynes: Open University Press.

Hazan, C., & Shaver, P. R. (1990). Love and work: an attachment-theoretical perspective. *Journal of Personality and Social Psychology, 59*: 270–280.

Healthcare Counselling and Psychotherapy Journal (2007). News item: Department of Health announces 11 new talking therapy projects. 7(4): 2 [available via: http://www.gnn.gov.uk/environment/ http://www.scotland.gov.uk/Resource/Doc/924/0051490.doc 31/7.07].

Henderson, P. (1999). Supervision in medical settings. In: M. Carroll & E. Holloway (Eds.), *Counselling Supervision in Context* (pp. 85–103). London: Sage.

Henderson, P. (2007). Topics in training. *Healthcare Counselling and Psychotherapy Journal, 7*(4): 27.

Hinshelwood, R. D. (1999). The difficult patient. *British Journal of Psychiatry, 174*: 187–190.

Home Office (2002). *Achieving the Best Evidence in Criminal Proceedings: Guidance for Vulnerable and Intimidated Witnesses Including Children.* London: Home Office.

Jung, C. J. (1982). *Memories, Dreams, Reflections.* Glasgow: Collins.

Karpman, S. (1968). Fairy tales and script drama analysis. *Transactional Analysis Bulletin, 26*: 39–43 [available via: www.kaprmandramatriangle.com].

Langs, R. D. (1988). *A Primer for Psychotherapy.* New York: Gardner Press.

Langs, R. D. (1993). *Empowered Psychotherapy.* London: Karnac.

Laplanche, J., & Pontalis, J. B. (1988). *The Language of Psychoanalysis.* London: Karnac.

Lewis, G., & Appleby, L. (1988). Personality disorder: the patients psychiatrists dislike. *British Journal of Psychiatry, 153*: 44–49.

Liddle, H. A., & Frank, A. (2006). The road ahead: achievements and challenges for adolescent substance abuse treatment research. In:

H. Liddle & C. Rowe (Eds.), *Treating Adolescent Substance Abuse: State of the Science* (pp. 473–500). London: Cambridge University Press.

Malan, D. H. (1976). *Frontier of Brief Psychotherapy*. New York: Plenum.

Mann, J. (1973). *Time-Limited Psychotherapy*. Cambridge, MA: Harvard University Press.

Martin, E. (2002). Listening to the absent patient: therapeutic aspects of supervision. In: J. Stewart, E. Martin, M. Banks & C. Driver (Eds.), *Supervising Psychotherapy: Psychoanalytic and Psychodynamic Perspectives* (pp. 11–22). London: Sage.

Mattinson, J. (1975). *The Reflection Process in Casework Supervision*. London: Tavistock.

Mearns, D. (1998). Future horizons. *CMS Journal, 57*: 1–5.

Mellor-Clark, J. (2000). A personal foreword. *British Journal of Guidance and Counselling, 28*(2): 158.

Menzies, I. E. P. (1984). *The Functioning of Social Systems as a Defence Against Anxiety*. London: Tavistock.

Molnos, A. (1995). *A Question of Time: Essentials of Brief Dynamic Psychotherapy*. London: Karnac.

Morgan, G. (1986). *Images of Organization*. London: Sage.

Mueller, M., & Riggs, E. (2008). Basic CBT theory, assessment and formulation (OCTC Workshop). Chelmsford.

Ogden, T. H. (2004). On holding and containing, being and dreaming. *International Journal of Psychoanalysis, 85*: 1349–1364.

Pearlman, L. A., & Saakvitne, K. W. (1995). *Trauma and the Therapist Counter-Transference and Vicarious Traumatisation in Psychotherapy With Incest Survivors*. New York: W. W. Norton.

Pines, M. (1978). Group-analytic psychotherapy of the borderline patient. *Group Analysis, 11*: 115–126.

Plato (1983). *The Last Days of Socrates*. London: Penguin Classics.

Reeves, J. (1998). Embracing the context—the supervision of counsellors in primary care, MSc (amended) (pp. 39–40). Bristol University.

Rey, J. H. (1979). Schizoid phenomena in the borderline. In: J. Le Boit & A. Capponi (Eds.), *Advances in the Psychotherapy of the Borderline Patient* (pp. 449–484). New York: Jason Aronson.

Riviere, J. (1936). A contribution to the analysis of the negative therapeutic reaction. *International Journal of Psychoanalysis, 17*: 304–320.

Rose, N. (2003). Neurochemical selves. *Society, 41*: 46–59, cited in Gray (2007).

Rose, S. (2006). *The 21st-Century Brain: Explaining, Mending and Manipulating the Mind*. London: Vintage.

Roth, A., & Fonagy, P. (1996). *What Works for Whom? A Critical Review of Psychotherapy Research*. London: Guilford.

Rowland, N. (2007). BACP and NICE: a submission to a House of Commons Select Committee Inquiry into NICE (National Institute for Health and Clinical Excellence). *Therapy Today, 18*(5): 27–30.

Samuels, A. (1986). *Jung and the Post-Jungians*. London: Routledge & Kegan Paul.

Sanders, P. (2007). Decoupling psychological therapies from the medical model. *Healthcare Counselling and Psychotherapy, 7*(4): 8–10.

Savoy Declaration (2007). *Therapy Today, 18*(10): 9.

Searles, H. F. (1986). *Collected Papers on Schizophrenia and Related Subjects*. London: Hogarth Press.

Siegel, D. J. (2002). Foreword. In: *The Neuroscience of Psychotherapy: Building and Rebuilding the Human Brain* (pp. ix–xii). New York: Norton.

Soth, M. (2007). Polarising or embracing? *Therapy Today, 18*(10): 20.

Stacey, R. D. (2003). *Strategic Management and Organisational Dynamics* (4th edn). Harlow: Prentice Hall.

Steiner, J. (1993). *Psychic Retreats*. London: Routledge.

Stewart, J. (2002). The container and the contained: supervision and its organisation context. In: J. Stewart, E. Martin, M. Banks & C. Driver (Eds.), *Supervising Psycho-therapy: Psychoanalytic and Psychodynamic Perspectives* (pp. 106–120). London: Sage.

Stiles, W. B. (2007). Theory-building case study research. *Information Sheet no. 55*. Rugby: BACP.

Symington, N. (1994). *Emotion and Spirit*. London: Karnac.

Teicher, M. H., Anderson, S. L., Polcari, A., Anderson, C. M., Navalta, C. P., & Kim, D. M. (2003). The neurological consequences of early stress and childhood maltreatment. *Neuroscience and Biobehavioral Review, 27*(1): 33–44.

Turner, S. (2007). Challenges in the treatment of PTSD. *Therapy Today, 18*(7): 15–17.

Tyrer, P., & Stein, H. (1993). *Studies of Outcome in Personality Disorder*. London: Wright.

Wampold, B. E. (2001). *The Great Psychotherapy Debate: Models, Methods, and Findings*. Mahway, NJ: Lawrence Erlbaum.

Waskett, C. (2007). How to cut the waiting list. *Healthcare Counselling and Psychotherapy Journal, 7*(4): 20–24.

Watson, Y. (2007). Research, market, close the deal. *Therapy Today*, May: 13–14.

Willson, R., & Branch, R. (2006). *Cognitive Behavioural Therapy for Dummies*. Chichester: John Wiley.

Winnicott, D. W. (1956). Primary maternal preoccupation. In: *The Maturational Processes and the Facilitating Environment*. New York: University Press, 1965.

Winter, D. (2003). Repertory grid techniques as a psychotherapy research measure. *Psychotherapy Research, 13*: 25–42.

INDEX